THE ADDICTION RECOVERY WORKBOOK

THE
Addiction
Recovery
Workbook

POWERFUL SKILLS FOR
PREVENTING RELAPSE EVERY DAY

Paula A. Freedman, PsyD

ALTHEA
PRESS

For general information on our other products and services or to obtain technical support, please contact our Customer Care Department within the U.S. at (866) 744-2665, or outside the U.S. at (510) 253-0500.

Althea Press publishes its books in a variety of electronic and print formats. Some content that appears in print may not be available in electronic books, and vice versa.

Interior Designer: Liz Cosgrove
Cover Designer: Amy King
Art Manager: Amy Hartmann
Editor: Melissa Valentine
Production Editor: Andrew Yackira

Illustrations © Medialoot/Creative Market, 2018.
Author photo © GoykPhoto, 2018.

ISBN: Print 978-1-64152-117-8
eBook 978-1-64152-118-5

To Alison and Chris

CONTENTS

INTRODUCTION

HUMANS ARE COMPLICATED CREATURES. We have
brains, bodies, and emotions that don't always cooperate with one another.
When things go wrong, we have trouble looking at the whole picture and
tend to focus on just one of these parts, even though it's not exactly breaking
news that our minds and bodies are interconnected. Although the concept of
"mind/body health" has been touted as the trendy new wellness craze of the
current millennium, humans have benefited from focusing on the mind/body
connection for centuries.

Western healthcare has been stubborn about looking at the bigger picture. For a long time, we have used the "medical model" of treatment, which
involves pinpointing a specific symptom and then treating it in isolation. For
just as long, addiction treatments did just this: They focused purely on the
person's drug use or drinking, without considering the context in which the
addiction developed. Unfortunately, we have learned that this method does
not work for long-term recovery because it only treats a person at the surface
level. To truly make change that is long lasting, we must go deeper and start
healing at the source of the problem.

As a clinical psychologist specializing in addictive and anxiety-related disorders, I have learned firsthand what happens if recovery does not address all
aspects of a person's life. I have seen people thrive in recovery when they are
living at a rehab facility, but then when they go back out into the world, the
stressors pile back on and they struggle to cope in new ways. Often, they have
not fully addressed the source of their pain, the factors that led them down
the path to addiction. In my experience, it is rare that someone develops an
addiction when everything else is functioning just great in their life. Most people have more going on underneath: a history of trauma, experiences of grief
and loss, disordered eating, chronic pain conditions, job dissatisfaction, family

tension, symptoms of depression, bipolar disorder, or anxiety. Drugs and alcohol are often just the parts people see from the outside. Treating at the surface level won't change what drove the addiction in the first place.

Addiction does not develop in isolation, but rather as part of a complex puzzle. To recover from an addiction, you have to look at the whole puzzle and heal each piece, not just the piece involving drugs or alcohol. This book will help you do that. You will look at your physical, mental, emotional, social, cultural, and relational functioning, and explore how to maximize your quality of life in each of these areas. The coping skills you develop to manage cravings, withdrawal, triggers, and other symptoms related to your addiction will be applicable across all areas of your life.

This book is written for people who want to have a rich, meaningful life without their addictions. While it is intended for those with alcohol and drug addiction, those struggling with general addictive behaviors, such as gambling, exercising, or video games, can also benefit from the tools in this book. It can be used in conjunction with a 12-step program or an inpatient or outpatient treatment program, or on its own.

Unlike some addiction workbooks, this one does not declare that relapse is a failure. It is important to approach relapse as a normal part of the recovery process. While of course we do not take relapse lightly, we also know that spiraling into shame after a relapse does not help you get back on track with your recovery. This book will teach you to forgive yourself, learn from the relapse, and move on.

Whether or not you have been through the process of relapse before, this book will teach you tools for recovering from past relapses without further damage and for decreasing your chances of a future relapse. It will also teach you skills to stop lapses from turning into full blown-relapses. These skills are drawn from evidence-based interventions, including mindfulness-based approaches, cognitive behavioral therapy (CBT), acceptance and commitment therapy (ACT), and motivational interviewing (MI).

It is unfair to expect anyone to succeed in recovery when they are thrown back into the same environment, situations, and emotional states that led to the addiction in the first place. You are more likely to find recovery sustainable if you focus on healing traumatic stress, practicing skills to manage cravings and urges in everyday life, and developing strong relationships. Real recovery involves a deep dive into all parts of your life with an attitude of openness and honesty. You will need to look at and restructure both your inner and outer worlds to fully support recovery and reduce relapse.

In my individual therapy work, I often tell my patients that my goal is to help them become their own therapist. We work together to help them understand what they want their lives to look like, and then take action steps to get there. I can provide tools, ask the tough questions, offer empathy and support, and help them troubleshoot, but they are the only ones who truly have the capacity to change their own lives. If you are in a 12-step program, you might find similar support and guidance from your sponsor. However, your sponsor cannot control your actions. No one can fight as hard for your recovery as you can. No one else values your recovery as much as you do. My goal in writing this book is to similarly give you the information and lead you through the recovery process to help you become your own sponsor, therapist, and best friend.

This might sound like a lot of work, but I think you will find that you already possess more resources and strengths than you realize. It's okay to feel skeptical, hesitant, or overwhelmed. Take a moment right now to look up at your surroundings, roll your shoulders back, and take a deep breath. Know that you are not alone. I have written this book to guide you through the tricky parts of your recovery journey, with plenty of rest breaks along the way. If you've made it as far as opening the book and reading to this page, you've already taken a meaningful first step.

HOW TO USE THIS BOOK

THE PURPOSE OF THIS WORKBOOK is to empower you to succeed in recovery and reduce your chances of relapsing. It will help you through challenges in your internal world by teaching you how to manage thoughts, beliefs, and emotions. It will help you through challenges in your external world by showing you how to handle relationships and high-risk situations and navigate everyday life stressors. It is designed for you to use on your own, or alongside other elements of recovery, like therapy, treatment, or a 12-step program.

This book is intended to be used in order, from beginning to end. It is organized into three sections. In part 1 (page 1), you will learn about the biological, psychological, behavioral, and environmental factors that influence addiction. You will also learn about the scientifically proven methods for treating addiction. In part 2 (page 43), you will focus on learning and practicing coping skills for recovery, including ways to manage difficult thoughts, feelings, and chronic stress. You will learn about how traumatic stress impacts addiction and recovery, and you will gain valuable tools for healing from trauma. Lastly, in part 3 (page 119), you will tie together the knowledge and tools from parts 1 and 2 to help prevent relapse in your everyday life. You will learn how to structure a healthy support system and manage your relationships, deal with relapse triggers, and live a meaningful and enjoyable life without being controlled by your addiction.

Throughout this book, you will gain practical tools for maximizing your recovery and practice applying new skills in your everyday life. You will also be guided through several written exercises designed to help you map out your recovery. If a particular section or exercise does not feel relevant to you, you may skip it or complete only the parts that prove useful to you. Conversely, if a particular chapter seems very relevant to your struggles, you may wish to prioritize completing that section. Some people find it useful to take a photo or make a copy of a particularly meaningful page or exercise so they can refer to it in everyday life. This can be a great way to remind yourself of the tools you've learned. You may also find it helpful to repeat some of the exercises as your life experiences and priorities change over time.

The material in this workbook draws from acceptance and commitment therapy (ACT), cognitive behavioral therapy (CBT), mindfulness-based cognitive therapy (MBCT), motivational interviewing (MI), and other evidence-based treatment approaches. There are many ways to effectively recover from addiction, and there is no single "right" way. This book gives you a variety of tools for connecting with your own individual thoughts, feelings, sensations, and experiences, and to help you increase your awareness of what those experiences are like. As you move through this workbook, think critically about whether each concept could be useful in your daily life. Remember that ultimately you are the expert on your own recovery, and only you can determine what works the best.

PART ONE

Understanding Addiction

If you're reading this book, you're probably sick and tired of feeling sick and tired. You are ready to focus on the things you care about in life, without using drugs or alcohol. Part 1 will help you gain insight about how your addiction developed, learn about the various options for your recovery process, and create a plan for staying in recovery for the future.

CHAPTER ONE

Understanding Addiction and Recovery

On your recovery journey ahead, there will be hills and valleys, bridges, tunnels, and forks in the road. This chapter will help you understand how you got to this starting point. Once you are armed with a solid understanding of how addiction develops, what it looks like, and how it is treated, you will be well equipped to navigate all of the twists and turns ahead.

Understanding Addiction

You may have heard addiction described as a brain disease. Or perhaps you have heard it described as a choice, a lack of willpower. In reality, it is neither a disease nor a choice. Addiction, like all health conditions (both physical and mental), develops from a combination of biological, psychological, social, and cultural factors. No single factor is responsible for "causing" addiction. Genetics and chemical activity in the brain influence a person's susceptibility to developing addiction. Psychologically, addiction develops as a way to cope with painful life events. Growing up in a

CRITERIA FOR SUBSTANCE USE DISORDERS

To diagnose substance use disorders (SUD), health professionals use a set of criteria from the *Diagnostic and Statistical Manual of Mental Disorders, 5th edition* (DSM-5). A SUD can be mild, moderate, or severe, depending on how many symptoms a person has.

Diagnostic criteria fall under four categories:

Impaired control

- Taking more of the substance than you originally planned to take
- Using the substance over a longer period than you intended to use it
- Wanting to cut down or stop using, but struggling to do so
- Spending a lot of time thinking about or looking for ways to get the substance
- Craving (an intense desire or urge) for the substance

Social impairment

- Your using interferes with your ability to fulfill roles and responsibilities at school, work, or home
- You continue to use even though using causes social problems
- You stop doing activities related to work, social life, or hobbies because of your drug or alcohol use
- You withdraw from family activities or hobbies in order to drink or get high

Risky use

- You use in situations where it is physically or psychologically harmful to use
- You continue to use despite knowing that your drinking or drug use is causing physical sickness or worsening your physical or mental health

Pharmacological criteria

- You develop *tolerance*, so you need more of the substance to get the same effect
- You have *withdrawal* symptoms when the substance is leaving your body, which you deal with by using the substance again
- You can be diagnosed with a SUD even if you do not experience tolerance or withdrawal.

household or community where people use drugs and alcohol to deal with problems can influence a person to develop addiction, too.

When someone uses alcohol or drugs frequently and habitually, they can develop dependence, meaning they rely on that substance to handle day-to-day life. Typically, when someone becomes dependent on alcohol or drugs, their using starts to impact different parts of their life, like job performance or relationships.

TREATMENT

The most appropriate type of treatment depends on a person's age, health, history, drug of choice, and the extent of their addiction's symptoms and consequences. For some addictive substances, withdrawal symptoms are severe, so it is recommended they go through a medically supervised detox process.

The highest level of support available in treatment is through a residential program. In residential treatment, individuals live on-site, either in a hospital unit or in a group home, or similar residence. This is often helpful as it takes the person away from the people, places, and things that were part of their drug use while they detox and learn new skills. A person might stay at a residential program anywhere from a few weeks to a few months at a time. Some research indicates that the longer programs are more effective at reducing relapse than the shorter ones.

Some programs allow participants to continue engaging in their regular life while attending treatment. Partial Hospitalization Programs (PHP) and Intensive Outpatient Programs (IOP) usually involve the patient spending several hours a day, several days a week in treatment, while still living at home and working or going to school part-time. If a patient is stable enough to live independently, they can transition to outpatient counseling or psychotherapy, where they meet only once or twice a week with a treatment provider.

Most addiction treatment involves a combination of individual support (meeting with a professional one-on-one) and group support. Some programs, especially those for teens and young adults, also include family therapy sessions as a standard part of treatment. While some treatments are completely focused on addiction, many others treat mental health symptoms in conjunction with addiction, since they typically occur together.

Several types of therapy have strong evidence for effectively treating addiction. It is popular for programs to use more than one approach, such as using dialectical behavior therapy (DBT) to teach coping skills for managing emotions, and motivational interviewing (MI) to help participants recognize the consequences of their addiction and stay motivated toward goals. In addition to these evidence-based approaches, other treatments can be used either on their own or as part of an overall treatment plan. For many people, 12-step programs like Alcoholics Anonymous provide the community support they need to thrive in recovery, and some treatment programs even require participation in 12-step programs. Other activities that are sometimes used as part of a treatment plan include art therapy, equine-assisted therapy, yoga, meditation, aromatherapy, hypnosis, or biofeedback. Many of these alternative therapies will be explored further in part 3 (page 119) of this workbook.

A NOTE ABOUT 12-STEP PROGRAMS

Twelve-step programs like Alcoholics Anonymous (AA) and Narcotics Anonymous (NA) have been pillars of the addiction recovery world for nearly a century. In the 12-step community, members learn and practice 12 guiding principles to recover from addiction and live meaningful lives without drugs and alcohol. Most 12-step meetings have a spiritual component, though they are not restricted to any particular religion or culture. When a new member joins, he or she forms a relationship with a sponsor who is already part of the program and who can help the new member to work through the steps. The main purpose of 12-step programs is to help participants stay sober and to provide a supportive community. For some, this community is all the support they need; others prefer to attend 12-step meetings as part of a more extensive recovery plan. It is common for someone to join a 12-step program while also attending a treatment program or working with a therapist or counselor.

Humans are wired to solve problems in two ways: avoiding and controlling. In the world around you, avoiding and controlling tend to be successful. For example, if you are disgusted by the taste of broccoli, you can easily solve this problem. All you have to do is avoid buying broccoli at the grocery store, avoid ordering dishes that have broccoli in restaurants, and if you are served broccoli, choose not to put it into your mouth. If you want, you can go through life without having to tolerate the experience of eating broccoli.

In your inner world, where your inner thoughts, feelings, physical sensations, and memories occur, avoiding and controlling do not work. For example, if you are upset by a certain thought, you cannot avoid the thought in the same way you could avoid the broccoli. In fact, the harder you try not to have a thought, the more that thought sticks around! Go ahead and try it: Do everything in your power to not think about a purple elephant. Did it work? If you found your brain instantly conjured up a purple elephant, you're in good company. It is human nature for thoughts to pop up against the will of the person thinking them. The same goes for emotions, memories, and bodily sensations.

The way our inner world operates is very different from the way our outside world operates. However, humans still try to deal with the inner world using the same strategies they apply to the outside world. When we have an unpleasant or painful thought or feeling, we try to get rid of it. When we have a pleasant or enjoyable thought or feeling, we try to keep or repeat it.

In ACT, the efforts we make to get rid of some feelings and hold on to others are called "experiential avoidance" (EA) and "experiential control" (EC). Since EA and EC happen instinctively, we typically don't realize what we are doing while we are doing it. Over time, if a person relies on the same EA or EC behavior repeatedly, it becomes addictive. Any behavior has the potential to become addictive, but more common ones include using drugs, alcohol, food, exercise, sex, television, video games, gambling, and shopping.

Even behaviors that seem "healthy," like exercise or cleaning, can become harmful if used excessively. In any given situation or phase of life, you may have turned to a variety of addictive behaviors, depending on what you're drawn to, what result you're looking for, or what is available to you. For example, people who struggle with eating disorders might use dieting behaviors to restrict or control food intake, but in situations where they are unable to restrict, they might turn to another behavior, such as purging or excessively exercising.

What makes a behavior "addictive" is the *purpose* behind it and the *role* it serves in your life. To identify the purpose behind your behavior, ask yourself "What is this doing for me?" Sometimes the purpose is to feel relaxed, stimulated, or soothed. This means you are looking to *create* an enjoyable or pleasant internal state. Often, this is the purpose behind using an addictive substance when bored. In other situations, the purpose is to distract, numb, or get relief. This means you are looking to *eliminate* an uncomfortable or painful internal state. Often, this purpose drives you to use when stressed or overwhelmed.

 ## EXERCISE 1.1 RECOGNIZING THE PURPOSES BEHIND USING BEHAVIORS

All behavior has a purpose, whether we recognize it or not. Otherwise we wouldn't behave that way! Here are some behaviors people commonly use to manage stress, feel relaxed, decrease or numb pain, cope with boredom, or create pleasure and excitement.

Write an "R" beside each behavior you have turned to for *relaxation*, a "P" for each one you have used for *pleasure/stimulation*, and an "N" for each one you've used to *numb* yourself physically or emotionally. It's okay if you write more than one letter beside a behavior.

- Alcohol _____

- Cigarettes _____

- Marijuana _____

- Painkillers or opioids _____

- Cocaine _____

- Amphetamines or methamphetamines _____

- Psychedelic drugs _____

- Having sex _____

(Continued)

- Watching pornography _____

- Masturbating _____

- Watching TV _____

- Playing video games _____

- Gambling _____

- Cleaning and organizing _____

- Using social media _____

- Shopping _____

- Eating when not hungry _____

- Dieting _____

- Exercising _____

- Sleeping _____

- Gossiping _____

- Cutting or harming yourself _____

- Using prescription medication in nonprescribed ways _____

- Isolating yourself _____

- Other: _____

  _____

  _____

Understanding Recovery

People who develop addiction are trying to cope with unwanted emotions in the best way they know how. If you are relying on drinking or getting high (or exercising, gambling, or any of the behaviors mentioned in Exercise 1.1 [page 7]) to cope with unwanted emotions, then letting go of that tool can be terrifying. It is hard to face the fact that the habit you developed as the "solution" to your emotions has actually become a problem. This is why many people cling to addictive behaviors long after they've become aware that the behaviors aren't helping them have the life they desire.

YOUR BRAIN AND BODY ADAPT

Dr. Brené Brown, who researches shame and vulnerability, points out that "we cannot selectively numb." This means that we cannot pick and choose which emotions we feel and which we don't. We can't choose to not feel fear, sadness, or insecurity, because those feelings are just natural parts of being alive. When we numb painful feelings, we also numb pleasurable ones.

On a related note, we cannot selectively cling to emotions. We can't choose to only feel joy all the time. We don't get to choose *what* our thoughts, feelings, and internal experiences are. However, this does not make us passive beings who simply exist while life happens to us. We have complete control over our behaviors and choices. While we can't choose thoughts or feelings, we can choose how we relate to those experiences. We choose how much *attention* we give to our thoughts and feelings, and how much we allow them to dictate our behaviors and control our daily lives.

In recovery, you might feel overwhelmed at first by the intensity of your emotions, especially the ones you used drugs or alcohol to suppress. For a while, it might even seem as if those tough feelings are the *only* emotions you ever experience. Drugs and alcohol light up the reward center in your brain. Regular drug or alcohol use changes the way your brain processes pleasure, making it harder to feel happy feelings without the help of a drug.

After you stop exposing your brain and body to mood-altering substances, you begin adapting to a new normal. You will start to feel the whole spectrum of your feelings. While this involves feeling tough emotions, it also involves feeling joy, happiness, and love. The reward for letting in the difficult emotions is the ability to also fully and deeply feel the enjoyable ones. In chapter 4 (page 61), you will learn valuable skills for handling the natural ebbs and flows of your emotions without relapsing.

 ## EXERCISE 1.2   HOW RELIABLE IS MY BEHAVIOR?

Choose any behavior you marked in Exercise 1.1 (page 7). It can be an "R," "P," or "N." Write it in this space:

The first time you used this behavior, how effectively did it help you relax, feel pleasure, or numb uncomfortable feelings? Rate its effectiveness on a scale from 0 ("I felt exactly the same as before I used it") to 10 ("It worked *perfectly*").

0   1   2   3   4   5   6   7   8   9   10

If you rated the behavior on the scale of 0 to 10 every time you used it, would it have the same rating each time? Circle Yes or No.

Yes   No

If No, why do you think this behavior is not reliable?

Has there ever been a time you were unable to use this behavior when you wanted to? Circle Yes or No.

Yes   No

What obstacles could interfere with your ability to use this behavior?

EXERCISE 1.3 OUTCOMES OF ADDICTIVE BEHAVIOR

To evaluate whether it makes sense to continue doing something, you must weigh costs and benefits. Think about what would happen if you used a behavior from Exercise 1.1 (page 7) repeatedly over time.

Choose a behavior you have used before. It can be the same one you used in Exercise 1.2 (page 10) or a different one. Write it down on the line below.

_____

If you used this behavior every day for **six months**, how would it affect your . . .

Physical health?

_____

Mental health?

_____

Functioning at work or school?

_____

Relationships with family and friends?

_____

Finances?

_____

If you used this behavior every day for **10 years**, how would it affect your . . .

Physical health?

_____

Mental health?

_____

(Continued)

Functioning at work or school?

_____

Relationships with family and friends?

_____

Finances?

_____

A NEW UNDERSTANDING OF RELAPSE

In recovery, people sometimes use numbers to measure success. In 12-step programs, it is common to reward members for the length of their sobriety with special tokens, and those who have been sober the longest are highly respected. It can be encouraging to recognize these accomplishments. However, it can also be difficult to cope with a relapse if it means you have to "start over" in counting your sobriety. Relapsing after being praised for a period of sobriety can lead to feelings of shame. In this mind-set, it can lead you to spiral back into drug or alcohol use and give up your recovery efforts because you've "already messed up." Humans are not perfect, and treating recovery as an all-or-nothing process does not leave room for being human.

If you used alcohol to cope with stress for a very long period, and then in recovery you have coped with your stress head-on, then turning to alcohol on one high-stress occasion does not erase the hard work you've done so far. It simply means that you fell back on an old strategy. If you label yourself a failure for one mistake, you are making a huge generalization based on a single incident. You are not accounting for the many instances in which you didn't turn to alcohol. While mistakes have consequences, they also don't give you or anyone else the right to dismiss the efforts you've made and will continue to make. Every moment is a brand-new moment, so treat it as such and allow yourself to move on.

Your likelihood of relapsing in the future will decrease if you approach relapse as a learning opportunity and a chance to make your recovery plan even stronger. The most powerful way to change your view of relapse is to practice self-compassion and self-forgiveness—we'll explore both of these in part 2 (page 43) of this workbook.

COMBATING SHAME AND STIGMA

Unfortunately, our society is not always kind to those who have struggled with addiction or other mental health disorders. People sometimes get stuck on a particular detail—like the fact that you have been to treatment, take medication for bipolar disorder, or have been arrested—and they make assumptions about you. This type of assumption is known as "stigma," and it can be extremely hurtful.

Stigma can present many challenges to recovery. Discrimination at a societal level can make it harder for someone in recovery to find a job or housing than someone who has no addiction or legal history. People who face stigma experience more shame and fear, which can take a toll on relationships, health, and quality of life.

Even if you don't face stigma from the outside world, you might judge yourself based on your struggles or things you have done in your addiction. You may be self-critical and have a hard time seeing your positive qualities. This can contribute to low self-esteem and make you more likely to put off getting treatment or reaching out to others when you're struggling. The judgments you put on yourself come from *self-stigma*: the belief that you are inherently flawed, bad, or a failure.

Stigma of any kind is recovery's worst enemy because it breeds feelings of shame. To combat shame and stigma, you need understanding, empathy, and compassion. When you point out and challenge stigma, the shame gets weaker. Talking about your experiences with a therapist, friend, or trusted family member can help you heal. You can learn to practice compassion for yourself through activities like writing letters to your childhood self and imagining how you might talk to a loved one if that person was the one being self-critical. We'll discuss these strategies further in chapters 2, 3, and 4.

As you find and connect with people who are compassionate and understanding, you'll begin to see that not everyone will judge you for what you've been through. You may even find in recovery that the relationships you form are more rewarding than you ever thought possible. Chapter 5 of this book (page 77) will help you establish and nurture relationships with people who are able to see you for *all* of you.

THREE KINDS OF STIGMA

Stigma is what happens when people have trouble seeing the whole picture of your situation, and they treat you unfairly or make assumptions about your character because of your past drug or alcohol use.

Researchers have identified three kinds of stigma. Each can create barriers to successful recovery.

Enacted Stigma
SOCIAL DISCRIMINATION AGAINST PEOPLE WITH ADDICTIONS

What it looks like:

- Not being hired for a job due to addiction or legal history

- Being denied access to housing

- Being rejected by family, friends, or acquaintances

Perceived Stigma
BELIEFS HELD BY PEOPLE WITH ADDICTIONS

What it looks like:

- Assuming that you are being judged by others

- Accusing others of judging you for your struggles with addiction

Self-Stigma
NEGATIVE THOUGHTS OR FEELINGS ABOUT YOURSELF AS A PERSON WITH ADDICTION

What it looks like:

- Feelings of shame, fear, and self-criticism

- Avoiding treatment due to fear of failure

- Staying distant from others or avoiding intimate relationships

- Failing to seek employment due to lack of confidence

SETTING YOURSELF UP FOR SUCCESS

Let's say you want to quit eating ice cream. You and your family move to an "ice cream-free" community. The grocery stores don't stock ice cream, and the restaurants don't serve it, so you never see it anywhere. You have a new job that's rewarding and fun, and no longer feel stressed like you did in your old job. It's sunny and 75 degrees year-round, and you have never felt more relaxed. Before you know it, you don't think about ice cream much, and your old reasons for eating it—to feel pleasure and to cope with stress— seem irrelevant.

Now let's say you're trying to quit, but you work in an ice cream shop every day and you typically eat ice cream to manage stress. Your husband and kids know this, so they keep the house stocked, and when they see you feeling anxious, they serve you a big bowl of the sweet, creamy stuff. You tell them to stop keeping it in the house, but they like it themselves and aren't willing to honor that request. You want to quit your job at the ice cream shop, but you can't find another one that pays enough to make ends meet. It feels as if you are doomed to keep turning to ice cream for the rest of your life.

In a magical fantasy world, you could simply eliminate relapse triggers from your life. Here on planet Earth, however, stress and triggers are par for the course. Knowing this, there are certain steps you can take to set yourself up for success in recovery.

Tips for Reducing Relapse Risk

- Build a support system, including your treatment team, therapist, sponsor, partner, and friends.

- Identify relapse triggers: people, places, and things associated with using.

- Consider avoiding situations where drugs or alcohol will be present.

- If you cannot avoid a triggering situation, be strategic. Bring a sober friend, and decide ahead of time how you will handle cravings.

- Keep resources like this workbook, a coping card, and phone numbers for the people in your support system handy at all times.

- Establish a recovery-focused daily ritual, such as daily meditation, group therapy, 12-step meetings, yoga, or other community-based activities.

CHAPTER TWO

Chronic Stress, Trauma, and the Nature of Relapse

As we discussed in chapter 1, addiction develops from an effort to cope with internal and external experiences. Addictive behaviors are often geared toward soothing physical pain, numbing painful emotions, distracting from or blocking out painful memories, or self-medicating. This chapter will help you understand how stress and trauma have influenced your addiction and contributed to past relapses. It will teach you to recognize and manage hidden triggers that often drive using behavior and to heal from the painful things you've experienced.

Stressors and the Reality of Triggers and Relapse

Remember the example in chapter 1 about wanting to recover from an ice cream addiction while working in an ice cream shop (page 16)? We cannot prevent being stressed, triggered, or overwhelmed in everyday life. Even if you can limit or avoid being in high-risk environments where your drug of choice is present, you cannot avoid feeling stress.

Every person experiences stress differently, depending on:

- How long the stressor has been going on

- How long you expect the stressor to continue

- How many times in your life you have experienced this same type of stress

- How many times in your life you have experienced other types of stress

- How you have learned to cope with the stress

- What resources are available to you for handling the stress

Let's look at the different types of stress—everyday stress, traumatic stress, and toxic stress—to understand how each one plays a role in addiction and recovery.

EVERYDAY STRESS

The hassles we encounter in everyday life inevitably create stress, which can lead us to feel irritated, frustrated, or even panicked. Even though your logical brain knows that these stressors are not life-threatening, your brain's fight-or-flight response system doesn't know the difference between serious threats and everyday hassles, so it still becomes activated. Some of these day-to-day stressors might involve unforeseen obstacles to your routine, such as a delayed bus, a broken household appliance, or getting stuck in traffic. Other less common stressors, like preparing to move to a new apartment, are not unexpected, but they still are frustrating.

Workplace stressors are some of the most common. The unrelenting pressure to meet deadlines, give presentations, or tolerate difficult coworkers can be exhausting. Juggling many tasks or responsibilities at once often triggers the stress response. If you are unemployed, the process of searching for a job can be stressful. Being fired from a job can cause overwhelming stress. Yet most people face these stressful experiences at some point in life. Acknowledging that this is a common type of stress can help you be compassionate with yourself when you're having a stress reaction, and since so many people can relate, you can get support from friends and coworkers.

Most of us also experience relational and interpersonal stressors. Your nosy neighbor, your pushy mother-in-law, or your sassy teenaged daughter will test your patience. Arguments with loved ones and misunderstandings with friends are natural parts of life. Stepping back to see the big picture can be extremely powerful in helping you take these situations in stride. While conflicts like these are stressful, practicing open and assertive communication skills will help you resolve them without panicking. With practice, you start to trust your ability to navigate these stressors successfully, and you don't have to try to avoid or control them. Chapter 5 (page 77) digs deeper into setting boundaries and managing relational conflict.

 ## EXERCISE 2.1 NAMING YOUR EVERYDAY STRESS

Think about the major areas of your life today and the stressors they involve. Some of these areas might not bring stress every day, since certain periods of time bring more stress than others (e.g., accountants experience higher stress during tax season). There's no escaping everyday stress, but pinpointing your predictable sources and times of stress will help you recognize where and when you are most vulnerable to getting overwhelmed and experiencing urges to relapse.

What causes you stress . . .

In your home?

_____

_____

In your family relationships?

_____

_____

In your friendships?

_____

_____

At work or school?

_____

_____

When it comes to your health?

_____

_____

When it comes to your finances?

_____

_____

TRAUMATIC STRESS

Although plenty of everyday situations trigger the stress response, in those scenarios your life is not truly in danger and your physical safety is not threatened. But there are life situations that are truly dangerous and can lead to serious harm to yourself or someone else—situations you may have already experienced. These events trigger what is called traumatic stress.

Trauma is an emotional response to an event or series of events where someone's safety is threatened, either physically or emotionally. There are many situations that can cause trauma, such as being in an accident, witnessing or being the target of violence, being the victim of abuse or assault, or being struck by a natural disaster. After a traumatic event occurs, the person tends to feel shock, numbness, or denial. Over time, the trauma survivor might have unpredictable emotions, increased fears, painful unwanted memories or flashbacks, or physical symptoms like an upset stomach.

The sidebar on page 23 lists symptoms of post-traumatic stress disorder. It is important to protect yourself when healing from trauma. Describing the details of your traumatic memories is something you should do only in a safe environment; it is recommended you do this work with a trained professional, like a therapist or counselor. Otherwise, you risk becoming retraumatized and overwhelmed by the memories. Engaging too much with the details of your trauma without proper support may put you at risk for relapse. As you work through the exercises in this chapter, please do not go into detail. If you wish to seek treatment for your trauma, you can certainly bring this workbook to therapy. There are Resources at the end of this book (page 159) to help you find a trained professional in your community.

TOXIC STRESS

The experience of going through prolonged, repeated trauma is called "toxic stress." Certain populations are particularly vulnerable to experiencing toxic stress. It affects children's mental and emotional development: Growing up in an environment where they are chronically abused or neglected or exposed to violence, addiction, or mental illness can have lasting effects on their emotional functioning. Children who grow up homeless, in a war zone, in extreme poverty, or in a community where gang violence occurs experience severe toxic stress.

PTSD SYMPTOMS

Post-traumatic stress disorder (PTSD) is a psychological condition that affects some people who have been exposed to actual or threatened death, serious injury, or sexual violence. Someone can get PTSD even if they didn't experience the trauma directly but witnessed it or learned about it. These are the main symptoms of PTSD:

- Unwanted and upsetting memories of the trauma
- Nightmares
- Flashbacks
- Emotional distress from exposure to reminders of the trauma
- Avoidance of thoughts, feelings, situations, and people that trigger memories of the trauma
- Negative changes to your belief system (believing that the world is a dangerous place or no one can ever be trusted)
- Negative mood changes (feeling angry, guilty, or fearful all of the time)
- Losing interest in things you used to enjoy
- Feeling detached from other people
- Inability to feel joy or other positive emotions
- Heightened arousal ("hypervigilance"), feeling on edge and scouring surroundings to make sure you are safe
- Exaggerated startle response
- Problems with memory, attention, and sleep
- Angry or aggressive outbursts
- Reckless or self-destructive behavior (including risky drinking or drug use)

PTSD can be diagnosed when these symptoms last for more than one month, and cause significant problems across different areas of your life (at home, work, and school). If you think you are suffering from symptoms of PTSD, please consult the Resources section of this book (page 159) to find professional help.

Problems with drugs and alcohol are common in people who have been exposed to toxic stress. Survivors of toxic stress often develop PTSD, but the memories and flashbacks that plague them might involve several events instead of just one painful event. They may also struggle to form healthy relationships and friendships, and may either try to feel powerful and intimidate or control others, or become dependent on others and fearful of being abandoned. If drugs and alcohol were regular parts of their childhood, they might start using at a very young age and assume it is the best way to cope with difficulties.

Situations that cause toxic stress:

- Recurrent abuse of any kind (physical, sexual, emotional)

- Ongoing and chronic neglect

- Having a caregiver with mental illness

- Having a caregiver with substance abuse disorders

- Living in a home with domestic violence or significant conflict

ADDICTIVE BEHAVIOR IN REACTION TO STRESS AND TRAUMA

Recall from chapter 1 (page 2) that addictive behavior stems from an effort to control or avoid internal feelings. The intense and overwhelming feelings triggered by toxic stress are some of the most difficult to tolerate. Additionally, the shame and guilt that some people feel after they have been traumatized are very challenging feelings. Further, the anxious feelings that come from everyday stressors can be tough to live with. It is no wonder that all kinds of stress lead people to relapse. Even if you mainly started using drugs or alcohol to *create* feelings like joy or excitement, rather than to *avoid* feelings like shame or fear, you may still find that difficult feelings lead you to think about using. As you recognize these connections, you'll become better able make an informed choice about how you want to respond to pain and stress.

TOXIC STRESS

Toxic stress is closely tied to addiction. Nearly one in four children in the United States is exposed to alcohol abuse at home. Children of alcoholics (COAs) are exposed to toxic stress that can have lasting impact.

- COAs are more likely than the general population to marry someone who struggles with alcoholism or drug addiction.

- Children of alcoholics are two to four times more likely than non-COAs to develop alcoholism.

- Children of alcoholics have increased risk of other drug use and are more likely than non-COAs to start drinking and using drugs earlier in life.

- Children of alcoholics are more likely to struggle with mental health problems and mood disorders.

- Having an alcoholic parent increases the risk of a child being abused.

A New Understanding of "Fight or Flight"

You may have heard of the stress response known as "fight or flight"—the activated state that a person feels when in a stressful, overwhelming, or threatening situation. This response has been a part of the human brain since primitive times. It developed to help us react to potential threats, like coming into contact with a wild animal, and deciding whether it was in our best interest to defend ourselves by fighting off or killing the animal, or to run away and seek shelter. Today, this part of the brain still alerts us to dangers in the physical world, but it also gets triggered by emotional threats, such as being bullied or emotionally abused.

Research by trauma therapist Pete Walker has found that in addition to fighting and fleeing, there are two more reactions we can have during this stress response: "freezing" and "fawning." In the "freeze" response, the person is too paralyzed by fear to make the choice to fight or run away. It can also involve dissociation, where the person loses touch with reality and feels detached from what is happening. In the "fawn" response, the person submits to the threat or goes into a pleasing and placating mode. For instance, when an abuser makes a demand, someone who fawns in response to stress will try to protect themselves by giving the abuser what they want.

None of these four responses is better or worse than the others, but the one you choose should depend on the situation. When used appropriately, each will protect you or help you survive a dangerous or stressful experience. Sometimes it makes sense to "fight" by setting boundaries, asserting yourself, and defending yourself physically. Sometimes it makes sense to use "flight" and leave a situation where you might get hurt. In some situations, the appropriate response is to "freeze" and stop struggling if fighting is not productive and running away is not possible. Being able to "fawn" involves pausing, listening to the other people involved, and compromising to end a conflict.

By understanding the four stress responses and recognizing which ones you rely on the most, you can start to heal from past trauma and respond more flexibly in future situations. Just because you have historically relied on a particular response does not mean it is your only choice. As you learn to calm yourself in the face of stress, you will be able to think a bit more clearly and decide which response is most helpful in a given situation.

EXERCISE 2.2 DO YOU FIGHT, FLEE, FREEZE, OR FAWN?

Here are some reactions typical of the four F's. Consider how you have reacted in times when you have been stressed, triggered, overwhelmed, or threatened. Mark each reaction you've experienced:

"FIGHT"

❏ Feeling and expressing anger or rage

❏ Intimidating other people

❏ Shaming or criticizing other people, speaking in a condescending way

❏ Lashing out verbally or physically

❏ Behaving aggressively toward yourself, others, or inanimate objects

❏ Treating others with disgust or contempt

❏ Defending yourself or others physically when attacked (but not initiating an attack yourself)

❏ Speaking up and defending your rights or the rights of others

❏ Setting boundaries

"FLEE"

❏ Running away or quickly leaving the situation

❏ Avoiding a situation that might be stressful or dangerous

❏ Constantly busying yourself

❏ Planning or obsessing over details of a stressful situation

❏ Hanging up the phone in the middle of a heated conversation, abruptly leaving the room mid-conversation, or blocking someone's messages

❏ Impulsively ending a stressful relationship (such as quitting a job or firing an employee without thinking through the decision, or breaking up with a partner during a conflict)

(Continued)

☐ Staying away from a place that you know is dangerous

☐ Staying away from people who have hurt you in the past

"FREEZE"

☐ Isolating yourself when a situation might involve stress or danger

☐ Disconnecting from other people

☐ Detaching from your emotions in a situation

☐ Feeling numb to any physical or emotional pain in a situation

☐ Feeling paralyzed and unable to choose a response

"FAWN"

☐ Doing what the other person demands

☐ Doing what you think the other person wants

☐ Going into "people pleaser" mode and saying yes to unreasonable requests so that the people asking won't get angry at you

☐ Staying quiet when you disagree, to avoid a conflict or avoid making a conflict worse

If you've been through something traumatic, especially if you've been traumatized many times from a young age, your brain becomes particularly sensitive to stress. This means you might get triggered quickly into that activated "fight/flight/freeze/fawn" state, even when there is no real threat present. You might misinterpret situations as more dangerous than they are. In that high state of arousal, it can be hard to think logically. This is a time when you are particularly vulnerable to impulsive behaviors like relapsing.

A person who is raised in a stable, loving, and consistent environment will be able to access all four of these stress responses flexibly and appropriately. When confronted with a threat, they are able to decide which response will serve them best. On the other hand, when someone has been repeatedly exposed to chronic trauma and stress, especially during childhood, they learn to survive by defaulting to just one or two of the stress responses. They are unable to choose which response would make the most sense in a particular situation, and they automatically use the one they needed growing up, even if it makes the situation worse.

 ## EXERCISE 2.3 EVALUATING YOUR RESPONSES TO STRESS

Remember that the four F's are designed to protect you in the face of threats. We are best prepared to handle life when we have access to all four F's and can choose which one to use. Sometimes the response you choose helps you get through the situation, but at other times your response can cause more harm. Recognizing each response will help you see where you should develop more skills. Use the following questions to evaluate the pros and cons of each response and learn what you might need to work on.

(Continued)

"FIGHT"

What situations prompt you to *fight* in response to stress?

_____

_____

When has it been helpful for you to fight in response to stress?

_____

_____

Which "fight" behaviors from Exercise 2.2 (page 27) have helped you?

_____

_____

When has it been harmful for you to fight in response to stress?

_____

_____

Which "fight" behaviors from Exercise 2.2 (page 27) have been harmful?

_____

_____

"FLIGHT"

What situations prompt you to *flee* in response to stress?

_____

_____

When has it been helpful for you to flee in response to stress?

_____

_____

Which "flight" behaviors have helped you?

_____

_____

When has it been harmful for you to flee in response to stress?

_____

_____

_____

Which "flight" behaviors have been harmful?

_____

_____

"FREEZE"

What situations prompt you to *freeze* in response to stress?

_____

_____

When has it been helpful for you to freeze in response to stress?

_____

_____

Which "freeze" behaviors have helped you?

_____

_____

When has it been harmful for you to freeze in response to stress?

_____

_____

(Continued)

Which "freeze" behaviors have been harmful?

_____

_____

"FAWN"

What situations prompt you to fawn in response to stress?

_____

_____

When has it been helpful for you to fawn in response to stress?

_____

_____

Which "fawn" behaviors have helped you?

_____

_____

When has it been harmful for you to fawn in response to stress?

_____

_____

Which "fawn" behaviors have been harmful?

_____

_____

HOW YOU COPE

People cope with trauma and stress in a variety of ways. Some people direct their efforts at *numbing* their feelings, while others focus on *distracting* themselves so that they can move on with their days. Lastly, there are people who cope by finding ways to *make sense of what happened* and learning how to feel strong and resilient as they continue to live their lives. In chapter 1 we noted that all behavior serves a purpose (page 7). Coping strategies are forms of behavior, and some coping strategies serve more than one purpose. For example, if you cope with stress by watching television, you might be simultaneously *numbing* and *distracting* yourself. There is no right or wrong way of coping. You can evaluate whether it makes sense to use a particular coping strategy by asking yourself "Does engaging in X behavior help me live the life I want to live in the bigger picture?"

If you habitually rely on the same coping strategy, you might find yourself in trouble in a situation where that strategy is not available to you or stops working for you. Many people find this to be true with their addiction. At first, drinking or getting high is a really effective way to manage stress. Over time, it stops working as effectively, or you have to do it more often to get the same effects. If drinking or getting high creates more problems than relief in your life—problems like strained relationships, declining work performance, financial stress, or health issues—then it is no longer working for you. The point of a coping strategy is to help you manage your problems, not to create more problems. The more coping strategies you learn and practice, the better equipped you will be to manage the many types of stress life throws at you.

As you learn to recognize the costs and benefits of your go-to coping strategies, you'll get better at choosing other options to include in your tool kit. This will also help you identify what you need in a given situation and respond in a way that will successfully meet that need. For example, if you are stressed about a fight you had with your partner, watching TV probably won't help as much as writing in a journal to process your thoughts and feelings and then talking to your partner to resolve things. This is a situation where clarity, honesty, and understanding are more helpful coping tools than avoidance.

EXERCISE 2.4 WHAT IS THE VALUE OF MY COPING STRATEGY?

Take a look at the table of common coping strategies. The list is not exhaustive, so several spaces are left at the end for you to fill in your own coping strategies.

Think of times in the past month when you have experienced stress. Place a check mark in the first column beside each coping strategy you used. Then, in the second column, write down the situations or feelings that you have managed using that coping skill. In the third column, write the immediate

COPING STRATEGY	I'VE USED IT BEFORE (✓)	WHAT I USED IT FOR
Went for a walk	✓	To get some alone time and a break from a stressful family visit.
Took slow deep breaths		
Called a friend		
Wrote in a journal		
Did artwork		

outcome(s) that followed your using that coping strategy. In the fourth column, write the long-term outcome(s). If you did not use one of these strategies this month, think about situations you *could* use it for in the future and fill in the columns based on how you imagine it could work. The first strategy row has been filled out as an example.

HOW IT WORKED (IMMEDIATELY)	HOW IT WORKED (LONG-TERM)
Gave me some peace and quiet, a chance to calm down.	Still had to go back inside eventually. The stress returned, but I felt calmer.

(Continued)

COPING STRATEGY	I'VE USED IT BEFORE (✓)	WHAT I USED IT FOR
Listened to music		
Did yoga		
Sipped a cup of tea		
Took a nap or slept		
Read a book		
Watched TV or a movie		
Went to therapy or a 12-step meeting		
Made plans with friends		
Other:		
Other:		

HOW IT WORKED (IMMEDIATELY)	HOW IT WORKED (LONG-TERM)

Healing Chronic Stress and Trauma

Though your painful experiences will always be part of your story, they do not have to dictate so much of the plot. There are many effective treatments for healing trauma. Research shows that trauma can be eased or healed with treatments such as trauma-focused cognitive behavioral therapy (TF-CBT), eye movement desensitization and reprocessing (EMDR), narrative therapy, and cognitive processing therapy (CPT). There are also several interventions geared specifically to helping people recover from both substance abuse and trauma. *Seeking Safety: A Treatment Manual for PTSD and Substance Abuse*, by Lisa M. Najavits, was "developed specifically for co-occurring PTSD and substance abuse"; it can be used for both group and individual therapy.

No matter what method you use to recover from trauma, two factors must be prioritized above everything else: *safety* and *stability*. To feel safe, you must do whatever is necessary to get yourself out of harm's way and into an environment where your personal boundaries are respected.

Stability means having the ability to calm yourself down when you get emotionally overwhelmed. Learning to identify your feelings and label them is a good first step. Once you know *what* you are feeling, you can express that feeling in a healthy way. You can also learn skills for *grounding* yourself, which involves bringing your awareness back to the here and now when you become activated by a trauma memory or flashback. You might practice taking slow, deep breaths, noticing all of the sights and sounds in the room, or repeating a phrase to yourself, such as "In this moment, I am safe."

Your willingness to stay engaged in the recovery process is a necessary part of healing chronic stress and trauma. Turning to drugs or alcohol can be self-destructive and can even put you in risky situations that cause you further trauma. Choosing healthy, self-compassionate responses to trauma and stress triggers will ultimately help you heal from what you have been through.

It is not easy to deal with the pain of chronic stress or trauma, but turning to the behaviors you used in your addiction only created more pain. Now that you are in recovery, you have the chance to develop self-compassionate ways to cope with pain. Self-compassion is about treating yourself with kindness— the way you would treat a small child or a dear friend. If someone you loved was suffering, you would offer them comfort and support. Depending on what they were experiencing, you might offer words of encouragement ("I know you are strong and will survive this") or a gesture of kindness, like bringing them food or offering a hug. These are compassionate responses to pain. These are the things all humans deserve when they are struggling, but those of us who have been hurt in the past do not always know how to offer kindness to ourselves.

Exercise 2.5 (page 40) will help you explore some new ways of coping with stress to support your recovery.

There is no question that it's painful and challenging to manage the thoughts, feelings, and sensations that arise in the face of trauma. It is natural to want relief from this pain. Unfortunately, there is no way to permanently prevent memories or feelings from coming up. While this may be hard to accept, the sooner you do, the better equipped you will be to heal yourself. Now you can focus your energy on coping in ways that are not harmful to your recovery, and on treating yourself with kindness.

EXERCISE 2.5 NEW WAYS OF COPING

For each coping skill, indicate whether you've used it before and whether you would use it in the future (regardless of whether you have used it before).

COPING SKILL	I'VE USED IT BEFORE (✓)	I WOULD USE THIS IN THE FUTURE (✓)	I WOULDN'T USE THIS, BECAUSE . . .
Taking slow, deep breaths			
Sipping a cup of tea			
Taking a warm shower or bath			
Lighting incense or scented candles			
Calling a friend			
Listening to a guided meditation			
Drawing, painting, or other creative activities			
Going for a walk or being physically active			
Writing in a journal			
Reading a book or magazine			
Listening to music, playing an instrument, or singing			

Coping Tips and Strategies for Healing Chronic Stress and Trauma

- Take long, slow deep breaths. Count to 6 on the inhale, pause, and count to 8 on the exhale. Your heart rate increases when you inhale and slows down when you exhale, so deepening your breathing naturally calms the body.

- Take a yoga class or find a YouTube video to guide you through a few gentle yoga poses.

- Listen to a guided meditation geared toward healing trauma (see Resources on page 159 for recommendations).

- Develop a soothing daily ritual. It can be as simple as taking five minutes each morning to stretch and relax or do a "moving meditation" like tai chi.

- Talk to a therapist, who can help you process your emotions and heal from trauma.

- Write in a journal about your strengths.

- Start a gratitude practice. Every day, write down three things that went well that day, or that you appreciate.

- Join a support group to connect with others who have struggled with something similar.

- Educate yourself on what's happening in your brain and body by reading some of the books listed in the Resources on page 159 of this workbook.

- The Resources on page 159 at the end of this workbook provides information on finding a trauma therapist or support group, helpful apps, books and articles, and much more.

PART TWO

Coping Skills for Recovery

True recovery requires intention. By now, you understand the purposes addiction has served in your life and the underlying needs it was addressing. The next step is learning to respond to those same needs in new, more helpful ways. Part 2 of this workbook will teach you to manage difficult thoughts and feelings, develop and maintain rewarding relationships, and handle high-risk situations without turning to substances.

CHAPTER THREE

Thoughts

Humans are the only creatures on the planet with proven capacity for higher-order thinking. This ability lets us communicate and relate in complex ways, but it also creates a lot of stress and pain that other species don't have to deal with. In this chapter, you will learn how thoughts influence feelings and behaviors and have the opportunity to practice recognizing helpful and unhelpful thought patterns.

Words in Your Brain

Thoughts are automatic, often random groups of words or images that pop up in our brains, but instead of treating them as random, we tend to give them meaning. Over the course of our lives, similar types of thoughts keep popping up, and we connect them to an inner belief system. When a thought feels familiar, your mind can classify it as "important" or "true," even if it's actually neither of those things.

In recovery, the patterns of recurring thoughts that have become established in your brain can threaten your efforts to change. Your brain might try to convince you that you can't handle a certain emotion or situation without using. It might tell you that you're a screwup anyway, so you might as well relapse. It might tell you that things will never work out, or that you're a failure, or that other people are "making" you turn to substances to cope.

If you used to get drunk or high to cope with painful thoughts or memories, your mind might try to convince you that you "need" to use in order to get some relief. Learning to see your thoughts as comments from different "characters" in your brain will help you decide whether to take them seriously.

FROM THOUGHT TO ACTION

For better or worse, our thoughts influence our actions. Most people believe they are thinking logically when making decisions; however, certain habitual thoughts can keep someone stuck in unhelpful behaviors. Luckily, researchers in psychology have developed strategies for overcoming these stubborn thoughts and fostering positive change. There are six stages of change: precontemplation, contemplation, preparation, action, maintenance, and termination. For more information on each stage, see page 48.

 ## EXERCISE 3.1 I WANT TO CHANGE

Over the course of your addiction, you may have thought many times about wanting to change. The following questions will help you to reflect honestly on your desire to change and where you fall in the stages of change model.

When do you remember first having a desire to stop (or decrease) your drug or alcohol use?

What were your reasons for wanting to get sober back then?

_____

_____

(Continued)

Have your reasons for getting sober stayed the same, or are there new reasons now?

_____

_____

How has your desire to stay sober *increased* since you first thought about recovery?

_____

_____

 ## EXERCISE 3.2 I'M READY TO CHANGE

Two factors must be in place for change to happen: *confidence* and *importance*. No matter how much you *want* to stay sober, you won't succeed if you don't believe you're *capable* of it—that is, if you're low on confidence. You also won't make a change if you don't consider it a priority—that is, if it's of low importance. Take a moment to assess where you stand on confidence and importance.

If committing to abstinence "forever" feels too overwhelming, don't think about this exercise in terms of *the rest of your life*. There's a good reason the mantra of recovery is "one day at a time": We have greater chances of success when we break things down into smaller, achievable steps. No one can predict what will happen in the future, so you can base your self-evaluation only on where you stand *today*. Think of how confident you feel *today*. Then revisit this exercise as needed to reevaluate.

On a scale of 0 ("no faith in my ability to stay sober") to 10 ("complete faith in my ability to stay sober"), how confident are you today that you are capable of remaining sober?

0   1   2   3   4   5   6   7   8   9   10

If you answered less than a 10, what would it take to increase your confidence level?

_____

_____

If necessary, what steps are you willing to take to increase your confidence level?

_____

_____

Ask yourself these questions to evaluate how important remaining sober is to you:

On a scale of 0 ("I don't care at all about remaining sober") to 10 ("Recovery is my biggest priority in life"), how important is it to you today to remain sober?

0   1   2   3   4   5   6   7   8   9   10

If you answered less than a 10, what would have to change to make recovery more important to you today?

_____

_____

If recovery isn't very important to you today (score of 5 or below), what is your biggest priority today? How does staying sober help or harm your ability to focus on that priority?

_____

_____

STRATEGIES FOR IMPROVING YOUR READINESS TO CHANGE

If you're low on confidence, you might need:

- **More support**: people you trust, who are not going to trigger you
- **Professional guidance**: individual or group therapy, chemical dependency treatment
- **More information**: what to expect from withdrawing, etc.
- **Skills training**: learning ways to manage cravings and other ways to cope with stressors

If you're low on importance, consider:

- Thinking more intentionally about consequences of *not* changing
- Identifying what *is* important to you in life and whether change will help you prioritize those things

Six Stages of Change

- **Precontemplation**: You do not feel it would be helpful to stop using drugs/alcohol and have no intention of stopping your use anytime in the near future.
- **Contemplation**: You start to see benefits of getting sober and are considering recovery, but you're still unsure. Lots of people stay in this stage for a long time.
- **Preparation**: You are ready to get sober. You're taking steps to start recovery, such as scheduling an intake appointment with a therapist, making a plan to attend your first AA meeting, or opening this workbook.
- **Action**: You are engaged in recovery and learning new skills to support a sober lifestyle. You are changing your behavior in observable ways, such as refraining from drug use, participating in 12-step meetings, and expressing emotions in a healthy way.
- **Maintenance**: You continue to use the coping skills you have learned so far, and your confidence grows. You're still engaged in treatment, but the information is becoming more familiar.
- **Termination**: You're less focused on recovery. You are still engaged in activities that support sobriety, but may check in with a sponsor or therapist only every so often. It is important to note that not everyone benefits from moving to this phase, as decreasing your support can increase your risk of relapse. Staying in "Maintenance" for the long term may be wiser for addiction recovery, while "Termination" is more suitable for behavior change that has a defined end, like training for a marathon.

What's Holding You Back: Thoughts and Beliefs

While treating depression, psychologist Aaron Beck observed that most of his patients were buying into inaccurate thoughts that made them feel hopeless. He began to point these out so his patients could evaluate them more clearly. Dr. Beck is known as the father of cognitive behavioral therapy (CBT), an effective treatment that involves changing your thinking in order to change how you feel and behave. The following sections will teach you how to spot unhelpful thoughts and deal with them successfully.

COGNITIVE DISTORTIONS

Your thoughts do not always contain accurate messages, but if you don't stop to look at them, you can accidentally treat them as truth. If you follow them blindly, they can influence your feelings and motivate you to behave in ways that are not satisfying. Certain types of thoughts, called "cognitive distortions," are especially dangerous if they go unchecked because they warp your perception of reality. The following are 12 common types of cognitive distortions (you will use the letter codes in parentheses in Exercise 3.3 [page 51]). As you read about each, consider whether your brain has ever chimed in with something similar:

COGNITIVE DISTORTIONS	DESCRIPTION	EXAMPLES
All-or-nothing thinking (aka "black-and-white thinking") (A/N)	Thinking in terms of "always" and "never"; seeing the world in absolutes.	
Should/must statements (S)	Stating thoughts as rigid rules, using words like "should," "have to," "need to," "cannot," and so forth. When "should" statements are about yourself, they usually make you feel guilty; when they're about someone else, they make you angry or resentful.	I **have** to go to the gym tomorrow. I **should** be able to handle my cravings by now. He **should** know why I'm angry.

(Continued)

COGNITIVE DISTORTIONS	DESCRIPTION	EXAMPLES
Mental filter (MF)	Letting a single detail color your perception of the whole picture.	*I would have had a great time at the park, but that crying baby ruined the whole day.*
Disqualifying the positive (DP)	Dismissing anything positive that happens, and holding on to the belief that everything is awful.	*Nothing good ever happens to me. Sure, I went on a vacation last week, but it didn't even matter because I was so stressed when I got back.*
Emotional reasoning (ER)	Thinking something is true because it feels true in that moment.	*I feel like an idiot, so I must actually be an idiot.*
Jumping to conclusions: Mind reading (MR)	Your brain telling you that someone is reacting negatively to you, even if they aren't acting like it. You may misconstrue someone's body language or tone to convince yourself that he or she dislikes you.	*He thinks I'm a jerk, I can tell.*
Jumping to conclusions: Fortune-telling (FT)	Predicting the future in a gloomy way and treating this prediction as fact, even though it hasn't happened yet.	*I'm going to relapse by the end of the month.*
Magnification (aka catastrophizing) (MG)	Exaggerating something that really isn't important or noticeable, in a way that makes you feel down on yourself or someone else.	*I got a parking ticket; I am such a failure.* *He botched this morning's presentation; he's so stupid.*
Minimization (MN)	Reducing to a minor detail something that doesn't have to be considered minor. Like disqualifying the positive, you may think certain positive things "don't really count," and even though you acknowledge that something positive exists, you see it as insignificant.	*Sure, I stayed sober today, but that's not really an accomplishment. I barely left the house so it's not like I had to work that hard.*
Overgeneralization (OG)	Seeing a single incident as an overall pattern of negativity and awfulness.	
Labeling (LB)	Overgeneralizing to an extreme, taking a single incident and using it to negatively label yourself, someone else, or an event.	*(After forgetting to call someone back one time): I'm an awful friend. (After someone forgets to call you back one time): He's a selfish person.*
Personalization (P)	Seeing yourself as responsible for causing something negative to happen, when you were either not the reason or only one part of the reason for it.	*It's my fault that my friend relapsed; I wasn't available when she called me last night.*

EXERCISE 3.3 **THOUGHT-WATCHING**

Set a timer for three minutes. In the following space, write down every thought that pops into your brain until the timer goes off. Try not to think about what you're writing. It's okay if you find the same few thoughts repeating, or if they don't make sense. Write quickly so you can get the thoughts down without stopping to analyze.

Now, reflect on what you wrote:

(Continued)

How difficult was it to just write what popped into your head, without analyzing?

_____

_____

What do you notice about your thoughts right now?

_____

_____

Label any thoughts that are examples of cognitive distortions. Use the "Cognitive Distortions" key from the previous section (page 49) to identify which types of thoughts you had and write the initialism that applies.

When you're struggling with thoughts about using, do this exercise again and see which cognitive distortions you can recognize. Naming the type of thought you're having can help you see it for what it is—just a thought—instead of letting it influence your behaviors.

CORE BELIEFS

In the first days, months, and years of your life, so many things happened for the first time. If you've ever watched an infant discover his hands, or taught a five-year-old to tie her shoes, you've seen the astonishment of discovering something new. As we go through life, fewer and fewer things blow our minds like those early discoveries did. By adulthood, we're seasoned experts in how the world works, because over time each new experience gets filed away in our memories with the old ones, and we start to see patterns and connections between different events. Pretty soon we've developed a set of core _beliefs_ that guide how we understand ourselves, other people, and the world. These beliefs give us a system of shortcuts we use to make educated decisions in new situations. When we encounter a new event, instead of having to figure out from scratch—_What's up with this?_ —we tap our core beliefs and make an appraisal based on the information we have stored.

Core beliefs develop early in life and are usually shaped by significant events. For example, if a young child is punished whenever he makes a mistake, he might develop the core belief *I am a failure* or *I am bad if I make mistakes*. Throughout life, he might work hard to be perfect at everything—or, conversely, give up easily if he is afraid he won't do well.

If a small child's cries are consistently ignored by her caregivers, she might develop the core belief *I can't rely on people to comfort me*. Throughout life, when she is hurting, she keeps those feelings inside, because, according to her belief, she cannot rely on other people to support her.

Core beliefs are stored unconsciously and have been ingrained so deeply in our minds for so long that we tend to rely on them as absolute truths. This makes it hard to see when core beliefs are not accurate or change them if the shortcuts they lead us to are not helpful.

CHALLENGING THOUGHTS

Most of the time, we walk around unaware that our thoughts are narrating everything that's happening. We're focused on what we're doing, what happened yesterday, or what's happening later. Throughout this chapter, you have learned about different styles of thinking that can bully you into relapsing. Now that you can spot unhelpful thoughts, it is time to practice disconnecting from their messages so that you can make decisions you'll be proud of.

Your goal here is to view your thoughts as simply words or ideas being given to you by some character in your brain. Each of us has a little "inner critic" that sits in a corner of our mind and tries to bully us with unhelpful and negative messages. Unfortunately, you can't shut up the critic forever, and the harder we try to get him to be quiet, the louder he yells stuff at us. The best you can do is to recognize that those messages come from the critic, *not from your true self.*

Some people are uncomfortable around hornets and wasps because they're afraid of being stung. Critical and upsetting thoughts have a similar effect on us. We don't like having them for fear that they will sting us. Thoughts cannot hurt us, though, since they are just words in our brains. Imagine that your upsetting thoughts are like bees without stingers. They can buzz around you all they want, but they cannot actually hurt you.

Write a thought that makes you feel upset or anxious:

_____

_____

_____

_____

Now, take the stinger out of that thought. Write the thought again, but in front of the thought, write the words, "The bully in my brain is telling me that . . ."

_____

_____

_____

Let's make this thought even less threatening. Scramble the words around and write a scrambled-up version here:

_____

_____

Next time you have an upsetting thought, try this strategy and see if it changes how you feel. With practice, you'll start to give less and less importance to upsetting thoughts.

STRATEGIES FOR TAKING THE STING OUT OF THOUGHTS

- Practice saying "My mind is telling me that . . ." in front of the upsetting thought.

- Say the first word of the thought over and over, 30 times. Notice how it starts to sound like gibberish. Do this with each word in the thought, until it all sounds like nonsense.

- Pick a cartoon character with a goofy voice and say the thought to yourself in that character's voice.

- Sing the thought to the tune of your favorite song.

CHALLENGING BELIEFS

Beliefs take time to change. For some people, core beliefs that developed in childhood may never fully go away. This doesn't mean you're doomed to believe and follow them for the rest of your life. It just means you'll have to keep challenging those beliefs and introduce new, more helpful beliefs to focus your energy on.

The beliefs that sabotage recovery are typically along the lines of *I am inadequate, unlovable, incompetent, worthless,* or *a failure.* Remember that all of these words are *subjective,* which means there is no way for the whole world to agree on their meaning or "prove" they are true.

Using the strategies from this chapter, you'll start noticing when thoughts come up that reek of an unhelpful belief. By recognizing when your thoughts reflect misguided beliefs, you can stop dwelling on them and stop assuming they're true. You don't need to listen to these thoughts and let them tell you how to behave. Exercise 3.5 (page 56) will help you learn a new way to talk to yourself, so that unhelpful beliefs don't dictate your self-image.

EXERCISE 3.5 BELIEFS THAT SERVE ME

We've investigated the unhelpful thoughts and beliefs that influenced your struggles. Now let's identify messages you want to believe. Perhaps you already have some helpful beliefs, but they're hard to see because they have to compete with the unhelpful ones. Read each statement and think about how it could help you. Write your answers in the space provided.

If I believed this, how would it affect my self-esteem, my relationships, and how I approach recovery?

"I deserve to be treated with respect."
My self-esteem:

_____

_____

My relationships:

_____

_____

How I approach recovery:

_____

_____

"I am a smart and capable person. I am doing the best I can with what I have available to me."
My self-esteem:

_____

_____

My relationships:

_____

_____

How I approach recovery:

_____

_____

_____

"When someone mistreats me, it is because they are hurting inside."
My self-esteem:

_____

_____

_____

My relationships:

_____

_____

_____

How I approach recovery:

_____

_____

_____

"No one can predict the future. Worrying that something bad will happen does not actually mean it will happen."
My self-esteem:

_____

_____

_____

My relationships:

_____

_____

_____

How I approach recovery:

_____

_____

_____

(Continued)

"Other people deserve to be treated with respect. Respecting someone doesn't mean I have to agree with all of their ideas or behaviors."
My self-esteem:

_____

_____

My relationships:

_____

_____

How I approach recovery:

_____

_____

"The world is full of variety. There is some good in the world, and some bad in the world. Some places are dangerous, and some places are safe."
My self-esteem:

_____

_____

My relationships:

_____

_____

How I approach recovery:

_____

_____

It's okay if right now you don't buy into these statements. For the purpose of this exercise, imagine you see the world accordingly and picture what effects it would have on your life. You just might start adopting a new worldview.

WHAT'S TRUE?

Looking at the stuff from your inner critic, you can see how your brain often gives you inaccurate thoughts. When you challenge thoughts, you can see whether they are just random ideas or were prompted by negative beliefs. To find out whether a thought means anything valuable, ask yourself, "What is the evidence for/against this thought?"

Let's say your brain tells you, "That guy across the park is smoking weed and it smells good; you should go and get some." You might respond with, "Thanks for your input, brain. That's an interesting idea. On the one hand, I do like the way it smells, and I miss getting high. On the other hand, I don't think I'd be so proud of myself tomorrow if I got high today, since I'm getting drug tested at work soon."

Remember that feelings are not evidence for a thought being worth listening to. Behavior is evidence. If you have the thought, "go have a drink, you're bound to relapse anyway," you might feel shame when you haven't even had the drink! Feelings are not facts, though. If your actions demonstrate that you are not drinking, you can trust that you have done what you'd be proud of later in life.

Tips and Strategies for Negative Thought Cycles and Craving Thoughts

- When a craving strikes, set a timer for 20 minutes and go distract yourself with any pro-recovery activity. Notice how the craving changes over the course of 20 minutes. Repeat this as many times as necessary until the craving subsides.

- Make a list of the books you want to read, then pick one and check it out from the library.

- Make a list of the movies you want to see, then pick one and invite a friend to watch it with you.

- Write down your thoughts in a journal or notebook. Go through what you have written using the strategy from Exercise 3.3 (page 51) and label any cognitive distortions.

- Practice the strategies to take the sting out of craving thoughts. Repeat each word until it loses meaning, write down and scramble the words, say the thought in a silly voice, and sing it to the tune of your favorite song.

- Write yourself a thank-you note from the perspective of your future self. Your future self is living two weeks from now, and that self appreciates that you chose not to relapse. Write about all of the things your future self gets to do because of your current self's decision to stay sober.

CHAPTER FOUR

Emotions

Difficult feelings are just a natural part of being alive. Since you no longer use drugs or alcohol to cope with these feelings, it is important to learn some new ways to manage them when they come up. Chapter 4 will teach you mindfulness and acceptance strategies for dealing with tough feelings without letting them jeopardize your recovery.

"I Want to Feel Better"—Emotions and Addiction

There are six basic emotions shared by people all over the world: happiness, sadness, surprise, anger, fear, and disgust. We also experience more complex offshoots of these emotions, such as terror, excitement, inferiority, exhilaration, and so forth. Much as we wish to control what thoughts pop into our brains, we try to control which feelings we experience. No one wants to feel their toughest feelings, and everybody wants to feel their favorite feelings.

Unfortunately, emotions are sneaky. The pleasurable ones tend to be most intense right at the beginning, and then they fade. Imagine you're enjoying a delicious piece of chocolate cake. If you love chocolate, you probably experience strong pleasure upon the first warm, gooey bite. By the second bite, the pleasant feelings are still there, but they're a little more predictable. The initial pleasure quickly changes into an effort to make the cake last longer, or you notice that you're thirsty and wish you had a glass of milk, or you start to think about something else entirely and don't pay attention to the forkfuls of cake entering your mouth. Then, when it's over, you might find yourself chasing the original feelings from that first bite, or feeling guilty for scarfing down more than your body could handle and giving yourself a stomachache.

On the other hand, painful feelings tend to last longer than we wish they would. Mark, a 35-year-old marketing manager, has always felt self-conscious and uncomfortable on social outings, but his boss expects him to attend all work-related social events. He discovers that a few drinks help dull his anxiety. He may arrive sober to the events, but as soon as his anxiety shows up—which it always does—he heads straight to the bar. Sometimes, he drinks so much that he can't remember details from his conversations, which makes him embarrassed the next day. He just wants a surefire way to make the anxiety go away.

This is the emotional roller coaster of addiction. As we've discussed, for some, addiction stems from desire to hold on to pleasant feelings. People often remember the rush of their first high. There was pleasure, but after that pleasure faded, they never seemed to get those good feelings to stick around. To get the pleasant feelings, they needed to use more or use for longer.

For others, addiction stems from desire to get rid of unpleasant feelings. Alcohol gave Mark temporary relief from the anxiety he felt in social situations. At first, it seemed like he'd beaten the system by finding a way to feel confident at work events. Over time, the more he relied on this strategy, the more drinks he needed to get the same relaxed effect. Even though he'd found a temporary fix for his anxiety, it would always return the next time he had to socialize. So on top of the anxiety, he had a new unpleasant emotion to deal with when he sobered up: embarrassment.

EXERCISE 4.1 WHAT FEELINGS POP UP?

To cope with emotions, you have to know what you're feeling. It takes practice to recognize them in the moment. Using the emotion wheel in Figure 4.1 below, reflect on what you would feel in the following situations.

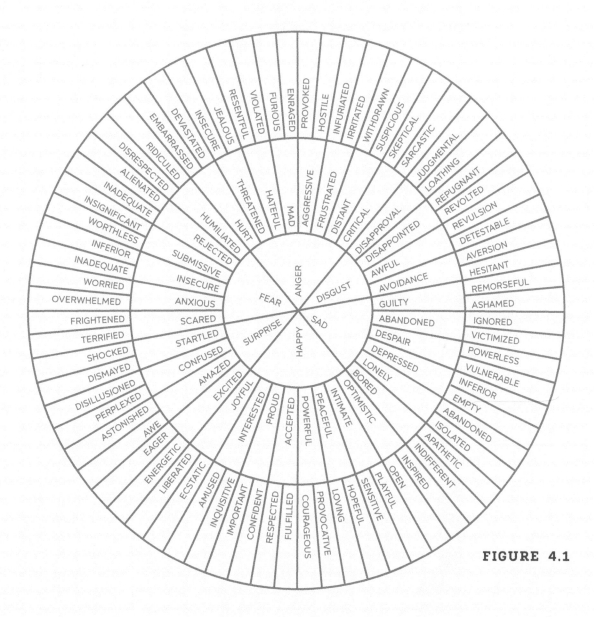

FIGURE 4.1

(Continued)

What feeling(s) pop up if . . .

I discover $20 in my coat pocket

_____

I wake up with a throbbing sinus headache

_____

I am going on vacation with friends

_____

A loved one just passed away

_____

I wake up from a good night's sleep

_____

I have a memory of the time I was hit by a car and broke my leg

_____

I just got home from an amazing first date

_____

A stranger sitting beside me on the bus suddenly vomits on my lap

_____

An old friend unexpectedly shows up at my front door

_____

My favorite food is cooking in the oven

_____

My boss yells at me for something I didn't do

_____

Notice that not every event will elicit a strong emotion, but you still have emotions, even if they're relatively neutral. Some words to describe neutral reactions include *calm*, *unbothered*, *relaxed*, *apathetic*, *stoic*, *or indifferent*.

 ## EXERCISE 4.2 WHAT FEELINGS MAKE YOU WANT TO CONTROL?

Think of the last time you had urges to use your substance of choice.

Where were you?

_____

What were you doing and who were you with?

_____

Use Figure 4.1 to help you answer the following:

What emotions were you feeling that day? List all that apply:

_____

What emotions were you *trying* to feel or *hoping* to feel? List all that apply:

_____

If it's challenging to remember what you were feeling, you may need to do some investigating. It takes practice to pinpoint what feelings come up, especially in high-urge situations. Next time you have an urge to use, try this activity and see what feelings are there.

DIFFICULT AND PAINFUL EMOTIONS

Think of your difficult emotions like pesky dogs, nipping at your heels. If you feed them, they'll stop for a moment, then bark louder and louder. If you let them bark without giving them attention, they'll eventually give up and go sulk in the corner. They might come back from time to time and start barking again, but when you stop rewarding their barking, you won't feel nearly as bothered by their presence. You also won't be wasting all of your food on their endless appetites.

Remember Mark's story from earlier? Mark quieted his anxiety with alcohol, and it worked about as well as feeding those pesky dogs. He relaxed, but the next time, his anxiety came back even stronger. The dogs will leave you alone while they devour what you threw to them, but as soon as they finish eating, they'll come back to bark even louder.

DISTRESS TOLERANCE

Mark believed he needed to drink in response to his anxiety. In reality, he had many choices for coping with his anxiety, and drinking was just one. He could have taken deep breaths to calm himself, talked to a friend or therapist to better understand what was making him uncomfortable, prepared himself to enter situations by reminding himself of his positive qualities, or worked on listening to others in conversations instead of pressuring himself to find something to say. He could have decided, on days when he needed some rest, to stay home instead of attending the events.

The challenge with these other choices is that they involve tolerating distress. You may believe that you cannot survive feeling overwhelmed or distressed past a certain level of intensity. When you feel upset, you may worry that it will just keep getting more intense until you explode. But rest assured, this has *never* happened in the history of humankind. Everyone who has felt overwhelmed has eventually seen it pass. Overwhelming feelings are not pleasant, but they cannot do anything to you besides give you a temporary unpleasant sensation.

An important part of tolerating difficult emotions involves describing them without judging them as good or bad. This is understandable; humans like to put things in categories, such as *bad = troubling, can't be tolerated, must be fixed; good = as it should be, can be left as it is.* But when we call something "bad," we're really just using a shortcut to say we don't like it, don't want it, or don't agree with it.

When you use more accurate words to describe your feelings, your brain handles those feelings more easily, since they aren't being interpreted as problems to solve. Over time, the more you use descriptions instead of categorizing feelings as "good" versus "bad," the less intense your reactions will become.

Exercise 4.3 will help you practice acknowledging emotions without categorizing them.

 ## EXERCISE 4.3 GREETING EMOTIONS WITHOUT JUDGMENT

See if any of the following phrases accurately describe how you experience the emotions in the list that follows them. Fill in the blanks with the body part(s) (chest, stomach, neck, shoulders, head, feet, and so on) where you feel the sensations. If you come up with a more accurate way to describe how one of the tough emotions feels to you, use your own words instead. You might find more than one description applies to a single emotion.

Nonjudgmental descriptors:

Feels like something heavy is in or on my _____

Feels like a pressure closing in on my _____

A tightening or tense muscles in my _____

A numbness in my _____

A foggy sensation in my head _____

A tingling feeling in my _____

A lump in my throat, a frog in my throat _____

A pit in my stomach _____

A ringing in my ears _____

(Continued)

A sharp or stabbing sensation in my _____

A feeling of heat or warmth in my _____

A cold or clammy feeling in my _____

A sweaty sensation in my _____

A buzzing sensation in my _____

A dry sensation in my _____

A strange taste in my mouth, like _____

Imagine what each emotion feels like and describe nonjudgmentally:
Panicked

_____

Terrified

_____

Ashamed

_____

Enraged

_____

Disgusted

_____

Other tough emotion

_____

Next time you feel one of these emotions, try to use these descriptions instead of words like "bad" or "awful." Notice whether your experience of these feelings changes at all as you practice this new language.

CLEAN AND DIRTY PAIN

Pain is part of being human. We break a bone, and it hurts. We get broken up with, and it hurts. A pet or a loved one passes away, and it hurts. It's natural for these experiences to create pain. The ACT term for this natural, unavoidable pain is "clean pain." Clean pain is any pain that arises from the experiences we naturally have as humans just by being alive. All of us have experienced clean pain in some way, shape, or form.

When pain happens, it reminds us that there are things we can't control. We don't like the way this feels, so we try to regain control by looking for ways to prevent future pain. Our brains think we shouldn't experience pain, even though it's natural. We treat pain as something that's wrong with us, or we call ourselves weak, especially if the pain comes in the form of a difficult emotion that we believe we should not have.

These responses to clean pain are examples of "dirty pain." *Dirty pain is any reaction to clean pain that we inadvertently create*, like beating ourselves up with negative thoughts, ignoring an injury and making it worse, or sabotaging our next relationship out of fear of getting hurt again. Dirty pain is also called "suffering." While pain is inevitable, suffering is a choice.

Dirty pain usually involves your effort to explain the clean pain, or to try to make clean pain go away. For example, you might make a mistake at work, and feel embarrassed. The embarrassment is clean pain, a natural reaction to the mistake. Then, your brain chimes in with criticism, saying things like *I'm so stupid. I shouldn't even bother taking on new projects.* If your emotions feel intense, you might have thoughts like *I'm overreacting. Other people have it much worse than me. I shouldn't be upset.*

Addictive behaviors are often forms of dirty pain or suffering. In an attempt to get rid of the pain from an injury or chronic condition, you use painkillers. In an attempt to cope with the pain of traumatic memories, you get drunk or high. These behaviors might feel like they really do get rid of your pain, but the effect is temporary. As soon as you sober up, the pain returns. In the case of emotional pain, it is only a matter of time before that feeling comes up again.

It is hard to stop trying to control pain. It means you have to actually FEEL the pain, which can be pretty uncomfortable, but there is a reward for doing this. When you accept that feelings are not within your control, you stop wasting your energy trying to get rid of them. Instead, you get to invest your energy in actions that will actually have a real payoff in your life.

EXERCISE 4.4 CLEAN AND DIRTY PAIN

In the first column, write examples of times you have felt physical pain, emotional pain, and a painful memory. For each, write down reactions (thoughts or feelings) you had at the time, ways you coped, and how effective those coping strategies were in the short term and long term. The purpose of this exercise is to help you recognize whether it has been worth your efforts to try to get rid of pain, or whether you ended up creating more stress or pain for yourself.

CLEAN PAIN	THOUGHTS AND FEELINGS I HAD	HOW I COPED	SHORT-TERM OUTCOMES (PAIN GOT BETTER, WORSE, OR NO CHANGE)	LONG-TERM OUTCOMES (PAIN GOT BETTER, WORSE, OR NO CHANGE)
Physical injury/ accident:				
Emotional challenge:				
Painful memory:				

What did you learn? Did you find a way to permanently erase the pain?

_____

_____

Taming Shame and Guilt

Shame and guilt can be so uncomfortable that they make us want to disappear. Guilt is the feeling of *I did something bad*. It goes along with regret after making a mistake, or doing something you consider a mistake even if it really didn't cause any harm. Shame is the feeling of I am *bad*, and is tied to self-worth. Though shame and guilt are unpleasant, they are not permanent feelings. Just because they pop up doesn't mean they have anything accurate to say. Recognizing and voicing feelings of shame and guilt will take away their power. Remember that these feelings are like those pesky dogs. They can bark and nip at you, but they cannot actually hurt you.

No one is "bad" at their core. Sometimes people do things that are hurtful or destructive, but there is always a more complete picture to see. You may have done things you regret, and it is natural to feel some guilt for these behaviors, but every day is a new chance to behave differently. Your story has more chapters to come.

SELF-FULFILLING PROPHECY AND SELF-SABOTAGE

You may have heard the expression "a self-fulfilling prophecy." When you believe something will happen, you can inadvertently set the situation up to meet your expectations.

Let's say you're convinced you will screw up a big work presentation. Your attitude while preparing for and giving the presentation can make your prediction come true. You might ignore the parts you do well and amplify the parts you fumbled. You might rush through the material to get it over with quickly. You could ignore all of your coworkers who are enjoying the presentation, and zoom in on your one grumpy coworker's expression. If you take this approach, *of course* you'll walk away feeling like you tanked it.

In recovery, self-fulfilling prophecy can help you or harm you. When you believe you won't stay sober, you might unconsciously sabotage yourself. You might ignore suggestions made by your sponsor or therapist, and refuse to practice new coping skills. You might continue spending time with people who use and hanging out in places where drugs and alcohol are all around you. Then, when you relapse, you feel like it was bound to happen. The problem with this approach is that when your expectations of relapsing are met, your belief that you will never recover becomes even stronger.

SKILLS FOR HANDLING EMOTION-DRIVEN URGES

In the heat of the moment, it is tough to try something for the first time, which is why intense emotions often lead to relapse. Drinking and drugging are old, familiar behaviors. You have had lots of practice with them.

To set yourself up for success, it is important to practice new coping skills when you are not upset. For the next couple of days, make a point of trying these skills when you are *not* upset, just to see what they look like in action.

Distraction comes in many forms. Count backward from 100 by threes. Try to write down the names of every teacher you had since kindergarten. Make a list of countries, animals, or foods that start with each letter of the alphabet. Come up with your top 10 favorite movies, TV shows, books, and songs.

Grounding involves any of the five senses. Some examples include:

- The "5-4-3-2-1" technique. Name five things you can see and five things you can hear right now. Then name four things you can see and four things you can hear. Then three things you can see and three things you can hear, then two of each, and then one of each. This gets harder as you go, especially if you are trying not to repeat any!

- Take a few slow breaths. Notice how the air feels cooler as you inhale and warmer as you exhale. Notice how your chest and abdomen rise and fall. Notice the sound when the air whooshes in and out.

- Press your feet into the bottom of your shoes. Wiggle your toes around. Notice the sensations you feel. Is the surface under your feet mushy or firm? Can you feel the pull of gravity as you rest your feet on the ground?

- Sip a hot cup of tea and notice the way the cup feels in your hands, the way it smells, the steam rising off the top, and the way it tastes. Notice the sensation of the liquid moving down your throat.

- Squeeze a stress ball, mold some Play-Doh or clay, or find a small object to fidget with. Notice how the texture feels in your hands. Notice the weight on your palms, the material it's made of, and the different shapes it can be.

• Eat a piece of chocolate or another morsel of food you enjoy. Savor it slowly, letting it sit on your tongue for a bit as you notice the different flavors and textures.

 ## EXERCISE 4.5 CREATING A COPING CARD

When emotions overwhelm you, it is difficult to think clearly. Keeping a coping card with you will provide a reminder of your options. Fill in the card with strategies you have tried or are willing to try when the urge to use drugs or alcohol strikes. Use some suggestions from this chapter, along with other skills you have learned.

After you have filled out your coping card, make a photocopy of this page to keep with you, or take a photo of it on your cell phone. You can also post a copy on your mirror or refrigerator door.

When I feel:

Here are six strategies for me to use

1.

2.

3.

4.

5.

6.

ACCEPTANCE

The key to dealing with natural, clean pain is **acceptance**. Acceptance doesn't mean you like, want, enjoy, or welcome pain (or anything else you "need" to accept). It just means you are allowing it to be a part of your current reality. It means you are willing to tolerate something painful or unpleasant for the sake of getting to be alive.

Accepting unwanted feelings helps you to disengage from them, and as a result, the unwanted feeling becomes a little less intense and overpowering. In order to accept the feelings, though, you have to stop trying to make them go away.

For many people, fear gets in the way of acceptance. Fear that if you let yourself feel worried or scared or cry, you will sink into crappy feelings that will last forever. I hope that by now you know this is untrue. The next time these feelings arise, pay attention to the calendar or clock. The feelings will subside and be replaced by different feelings. Feelings don't need fixing; they just need time to pass.

KINDNESS

If you get angry with yourself for having difficult emotions, you will only amplify those emotions. Imagine there is a small child who is feeling scared, and it's your job to help that child get through his feelings without beating himself up. You might offer him a hug, encourage him, or let him know that it's normal to feel scared sometimes. If you tell him to "get over it" or "snap out of it," he is only going to feel worse. To truly help him through this, you need to approach him with kindness.

Adults are no different than children when it comes to the care we need. When we are harsh and self-critical, we only make ourselves feel worse. When we are encouraging and forgiving to ourselves, we can let go of self-judgment and find our way through those difficult emotions.

LOVING-KINDNESS MEDITATION

Loving-kindness meditation is a simple way to offer kindness to yourself and other people.

Close your eyes and bring to mind an image that is warming and comforting, like a bright ray of sunshine beaming through an open window. Imagine that this image contains all of the well wishes in the world.

Next, bring to mind someone you love. It can be a family member, partner, friend, or pet. They do not have to be alive. Picture that you are sending this ray of light from yourself to shine upon this person, while you repeat these phrases:

I appreciate your life.

I am grateful for the beauty you bring to the world.

May you be free from suffering.

May you feel peace.

If these phrases don't resonate for you, come up with your own expressions for sending positive energy and love to this person.

Notice any sensations of softening or openness in your heart area as you focus on sending warmth to this person.

Repeat these messages for several minutes, sending loving-kindness and warm wishes to as many people as you'd like. You can send it to people you do not know very well, people who have harmed you, or entire groups of people anywhere in the world.

Lastly, turn your attention toward yourself. Breathe deeply as you offer yourself compassion through repeating the following phrases:

I appreciate this life.

I appreciate my strength.

I appreciate my dedication to recovery.

May I live a life of meaning and purpose.

May I be free from suffering.

When Difficult Emotions Cause Cravings: Tips and Strategies

- Name the emotion. Draw or paint what it feels like. Use as many colors, textures, and shapes as you need.

  ....

- Pull out the coping card you created in Exercise 4.5 (page 73) and use a skill from it.

  ....

- Write down things you appreciate in your life today. If it feels like there's nothing, go back to basics: Do you have food to eat, a roof over your head, legs that work, or lungs that breathe properly?

  ....

- Scan your surroundings and name every blue thing you can see. Then pick your favorite color and do this exercise again.

  ....

- Notice all of the sounds you can hear in your surroundings. Notice any smells you can detect.

  ....

- Move your body. Go for a walk or run, do 10 pushups, or get friends together to play a sport.

  ....

- Read a book, watch TV or a movie, or do a puzzle. Notice the feelings changing over time. Notice if the feeling is less intense once the movie or story is over.

  ....

- Tear pages out of magazines and make a collage that describes how you're feeling.

  ....

CHAPTER FIVE

Relationships

Humans are social creatures. Research shows that social isolation can lead to all sorts of physical and mental health issues. In recovery, it is more important than ever to invest in high-quality relationships. This chapter will help you develop supportive relationships and learn skills for working through conflicts.

Relationships and Recovery: Social Health

Whether we're a social butterfly or a homebody, we all need to feel connected to others. Sometimes you need someone to hold you accountable. They might step in as the voice of reason when the logical part of your mind has been hijacked by your inner critic or thoughts of using, and they can distract you while you wait for cravings to pass. At other times you need a shoulder to lean on or a space to vent. In everyday life, you need people to laugh with, enjoy activities with, or even just to sit quietly beside you on the couch.

Remember that recovery involves looking at all of the pieces of the puzzle. Try taking a closer look at your relationships to see how the social puzzle piece fits in with the larger picture of your recovery.

WHO IS ON YOUR TEAM?

It's a familiar expression: You are a reflection of the company you keep. The people most familiar to you naturally influence how you move through life.

It's important to surround yourself with people who possess the qualities you value. For some, honesty is a priority, so they seek friends who are always direct, even when it means hearing something they don't enjoy hearing. For others, a sense of humor is vital, and they don't connect with friends who are serious all of the time.

One reason that 12-step programs are so popular is because they provide a community. When you're surrounded by people who are also committed to recovery, you know that you're not alone; there are people who understand the challenges you're working through.

In recovery, relationships that were based primarily on getting or using drugs or alcohol together can get tested. If you're in recovery but your friend is still using, you will likely experience a shift in the friendship. You may learn that the only common ground you shared was using. Discovering that a friendship is not as deep as you thought it was can be painful and confusing, but it is a natural part of the recovery process.

Some of your other relationships may have suffered during your addiction. Friends and family may struggle to trust you if you have disappointed them in the past. There is truth in the old cliché that time heals all wounds. Though it may not heal *all* wounds, the passage of time can make a huge difference. The longer you show your loved ones that you're serious about recovery, the more reasons you'll give them to trust you. If you care about someone, then your patience while they let their guard down will be worth it in the end.

EXERCISE 5.1 QUALITIES I VALUE IN OTHERS

Write the name of someone you enjoy being around:

What qualities do you like about this person?

What personality traits or habits make this person a good influence on you?

How can this person support your recovery?

Who else do you know who shares these qualities?

Use your responses to decide which social relationships you want to prioritize in recovery.

WHO ARE YOUR RECOVERY CHEERLEADERS?

Earlier chapters in this workbook focused on how all behavior serves a purpose. Similarly, all relationships in your life serve a purpose. Some people are in your life to help you let loose and have fun. Others are there for the serious stuff. No single person can meet *all* of your needs, *all* of the time, so it's important to have a variety of relationships. Relying on the same person for everything in life and disconnecting from everyone else can lead to a toxic or codependent relationship (more on this shortly in "High-Risk and Toxic Relationships" [page 82]).

One important purpose of relationships is to support you. In recovery, you want to connect with people who not only care about your well-being but also are invested in making sure you care about your well-being. These are your "recovery cheerleaders." They can include your partner, friends, family members, therapist, case manager, and other members of your treatment team. They can also include mentors, like a sponsor, boss, or spiritual leader.

EXERCISE 5.2 WHO SUPPORTS MY RECOVERY?

This exercise will help you identify people in your support system. Knowing who supports your recovery will allow you to know who to turn to in times of struggle to help you avoid relapse.

Who makes you feel proud to be in recovery?

_____

_____

Who are you willing to call if you have urges to relapse?

_____

_____

Who do you want to start spending more time with in your recovery?

_____

_____

Who can you count on to share wisdom, guidance, or advice?

_____

_____

Who is it easiest to be yourself around?

_____

_____

If you responded to several questions with the same few names, these are your "recovery cheerleaders." If you struggled to name anyone, don't be discouraged. This just means it is time for you to be intentional about seeking support. Attend group meetings or informal gatherings and see who you connect with. A therapist can help you recognize supportive people in your life and learn to ask them for what you need. The Resources section at the end of this book (page 159) has suggestions for meeting supportive recovery-focused people.

HIGH-RISK AND TOXIC RELATIONSHIPS

High-risk relationships are those that put you at risk of relapsing, whether they cause you stress, make you feel negatively about yourself, or expose you to risky situations—or all of the above! Some of these relationships are *toxic*, meaning the person is manipulative or abusive. They might feel insecure about their own struggles, and seeing you in recovery feels threatening, so they try to sabotage your efforts to stay sober. They might judge you, call you "lame" for not using, or try to remind you of how much fun they insist you had when you were using. Remember that people who truly care about you will want you to stay in recovery. A friend who tries to sabotage your recovery is probably not the type of friend you are looking for at this stage of your life.

If you're concerned about a friend's drinking or drug use, you may wish to help them begin recovery, as long as doing this doesn't put you in risky situations. Invite them to attend a meeting or group with you, or simply spend time together while sober to create a friendship that doesn't revolve around using. As you know, recovery doesn't happen until someone is ready for it. While you might motivate someone to take action, they have to get there on their own. To protect yourself, it is wise to keep a distance from anyone who is still actively engaged in an addiction while you focus on recovery.

EXERCISE 5.3 SPOTTING MY HIGH-RISK RELATIONSHIPS

Reflect on people in your life who say or do things that cause you stress or negatively impact your self-esteem. Write their names here:

_____

_____

_____

_____

Now reflect on people who have influenced your using behavior in the past. Write their names here:

_____

_____

_____

_____

Which of these people are you willing to ask to change their behavior?

_____

_____

_____

_____

Who could put you at risk of relapse? Why?

_____

_____

_____

_____

The people you named are your high-risk relationships. If you talk to them and their behavior still doesn't change, it is smart to distance yourself for a while. It's okay if you don't tell them why you are staying distant for now.

SOCIAL FACTORS AND RELAPSE

Research shows that relapse is frequently tied to social factors, including:

- Being in a violent or abusive relationship

- Spending time with friends or family members who abuse drugs or alcohol

- Feeling rejected by friends

- Going through divorce or a breakup

- The death of a loved one

- Living in a family where emotions are punished or dismissed

On the flip side, social factors that protect you from relapse include:

- Having a strong social circle of people who support recovery

- Regularly checking in with a therapist, sponsor, or treatment team

- Participating in support groups and attending 12-step meetings

WEEDING YOUR SOCIAL GARDEN

You *always* have a choice about whether to engage with someone. When a person has been in your life for a long time, it can be difficult to admit that they are harmful to your recovery. But you're not stuck with anyone for all of eternity, even if that's the message you've received from family or society. If someone in your life consistently bulldozes your feelings and needs, you have every right to limit contact with that person.

Since addiction often has a genetic component, you may have family members going through similar struggles. Depending on your relationship and where they are in their recovery process, they could either be great supports or put you at risk.

It is wise to approach relationships flexibly, rather than seeing them as all or nothing. Sometimes, if you ask the person to change his or her behavior, you'll get positive results. However, if they continue ignoring your needs, you may want to take a step back. While staying distant from a family member can impact the whole family dynamic, it may be necessary for your sobriety. The same goes for friendships that threaten your recovery.

Keeping your distance does not have to be permanent. If that friend or family member is able to change his or her behavior down the road, you can decide then if you would like to reestablish the relationship.

Healthy Relationships

Some crucial elements of healthy relationships include:

- Treating one another with kindness, consideration, and respect, even when you have differences of opinion

- Not taking advantage of the other person or intentionally hurting them

- No abuse of any power difference (such as boss/employee or parent/child)

- Not shutting down or dismissing the other person's feelings

- Apologizing for mistakes or misunderstandings

One key to a healthy relationship is *mutual respect*. This means you see qualities in the other person that you value, and they see qualities they value in you. Having respect for someone doesn't mean you agree on everything, but you are able to treat one another with kindness even in the face of disagreements.

THE MOST IMPORTANT RELATIONSHIP

There is one person in your life who has been there from day one, who knows you better than anyone else: you! It may sound cheesy, but the most important relationship you've got is the one you have with yourself. Even if you tell someone else all of your inner thoughts and feelings, they will never fully understand what it's like to *be you*. This means that you are in the position to be your own biggest advocate, cheerleader, and best friend.

In the depths of addiction, you may not have been a very good friend to yourself. When you're using, you are giving your power to drugs or alcohol. Over time, your drug of choice takes on the role of an abusive partner, controlling your every move and dominating your life. It crowds out your other priorities, and there is no space to invest in anyone or anything else. To reclaim your power in recovery, you will need to cut the ties to that abusive relationship and remind yourself that you are the one in charge here.

Exercise 5.4 will help you increase your self-compassion.

 ## EXERCISE 5.4 **A NOTE OF COMPASSION**

Write down something you dislike about yourself or that makes you feel ashamed, insecure, inferior, or embarrassed. Maybe it's a mistake you've made, a quality you dislike in yourself, or a flaw you see in your looks, body, intelligence, job, relationship, or anything else.

_____

_____

Next, imagine that you have a friend with this same flaw or who has made this same mistake. If it feels strange to write to an imaginary friend, picture instead that you have a child who has the flaw or made the mistake. This is a person you love unconditionally. You see this person completely, including their strengths and weaknesses, and you don't judge them. You forgive this person for being messy and imperfect. You don't blame this person for the cards they were dealt in life, and you believe this person has been trying their best to get through life as well as they can. Write this person a letter, telling them that their flaw does not make them a terrible human being and reminding them that no one is perfect. Make sure you also tell them what it feels like to hear them saying harsh and mean things about themselves:

_____

_____

_____

_____

_____

_____

_____

_____

What suggestions would you make to help them deal with their insecurity?
Remember, you love this person unconditionally, so any suggestions you
make will be encouraging and not judgmental.

_____

_____

_____

_____

Lastly, read back over your responses, and acknowledge that they're actually
meant for you. Notice your reactions to reading compassionate words directed
toward yourself. In the mix of feelings, you may identify empathy, sadness,
confusion—and maybe some others?

Take some time away from this exercise, and revisit it later. Read your
words again and allow them to resonate. Be open to any compassionate feelings that arise. If this is difficult, know you can return to this message at any
time for self-support in your journey to recovery.

Many people can easily point out what they dislike about themselves but struggle to see their strengths. It can feel awkward to acknowledge something you did well, but getting more comfortable with this is vital for building self-esteem. There is a major difference between recognizing your strengths and being cocky. In fact, being kind to yourself will actually help you be kinder to other people. Exercise 5.5 is designed to help you connect with your strengths.

 ## EXERCISE 5.5 RECOGNIZING MY POSITIVE QUALITIES

Answer the following without overthinking.

My proudest accomplishment has been:

_____

_____

I am happiest when:

_____

_____

My favorite of my physical features is:

_____

_____

Something I've done that I didn't think I could do was:

_____

_____

If you asked my best friend what qualities they like about me, they would say (if you don't know, ask a friend to answer this!):

_____

A gesture of kindness I've done for someone else was:

_____

_____

If you found this exercise difficult, do it again in one or two weeks. It may still feel awkward, but with practice you will get used to saying kind things about yourself. It's not as if you are broadcasting these statements on a billboard—you're simply acknowledging them in your own head. Validating yourself helps you build a healthy, stable identity, which in turn helps you build healthy, rewarding relationships with other people.

COMMUNICATION

We teach people how to treat us. When you are passive, people learn that you will agree to their demands. When you are aggressive, people might fear you or avoid expressing their true feelings to you. Everyone wants to be treated with respect, but many of us struggle to communicate in ways that are respectful both to ourselves and to others, especially in conflict situations.

There are four fundamental styles of communication (each may have variants). Most people have used each of the four at various times, even if they tend toward one style more than the others.

THE FOUR COMMUNICATION STYLES

Passive communication is about avoiding confrontation at all costs. Passive people deny their needs and preferences and defer to what others need or want. Typical signs are:

- Wanting to please others, seem easygoing, or minimize conflict

- Having a hard time saying "no" to a request, even if it's something you don't want to do

Aggressive communication is about getting your way. Aggressive people believe their needs are more important than others', and they use power, intimidation, or threats to get what they want. Typical signs are:

- Making demands, rather than requests

- Not listening to other people's perspectives

- Using power to control people when in a position of authority

- Nonverbal cues: speaking loudly, using a demanding tone, and staring intently to try to intimidate

Passive-aggressive communication is about getting your way while avoiding confrontation. It combines elements of the passive and aggressive styles. Typical signs are:

- Saying one thing but doing the opposite

- Knowing what they want but struggling to stand up for it or express dissatisfaction

- Wanting to please others while still getting their needs met

- Nonverbal cues: sarcasm, muttering under the breath, "forgetting" to follow through on a promise they didn't truly want to make, "accidentally" sabotaging a plan they didn't truly support, or giving someone the silent treatment instead of telling them why they are mad

Lastly, **assertive** communication is about treating yourself and other people with respect. It is about believing that your needs and other people's needs are equally important. The assertive style is generally most effective for handling conflict situations without taking a toll on your relationships. Typical signs are:

- Speaking clearly and directly in conflict situations

- Standing up for yourself without attacking others

- Standing firm on beliefs without trying to convince other people they are wrong

- Nonverbal cues: relaxed posture, casual body language, neutral or friendly facial expressions, a tone of voice that is confident but not pushy, making eye contact but not glaring

The basic approach to assertive communication is to use "I" statements, which start with "I feel," "I need," or "I would like," and then address a specific behavior. When you start a statement with "you," the recipient is likely to feel attacked and respond defensively. Consider the difference between:

"You need to stop smacking your gum!" and "I feel anxious when you smack your gum. Will you please stop?"

The message is the same, but the first delivery is more likely to elicit a defensive response. No one likes being told what to do, and they don't *need* to do anything just because you want them to. The second delivery is assertive; you are stating how you are affected by the other person's behavior, and it is clear what you would like them to do, but you communicate it in a respectful way.

Recognizing when you're using one of the less helpful styles and shifting to an assertive approach will help you navigate conflicts in ways you can feel proud of. Exercise 5.6 (page 92) will help you identify situations to pay attention to as you build assertiveness skills.

EXERCISE 5.6: WHEN DO I STRUGGLE WITH ASSERTIVENESS?

When and where are you most . . .

Passive?

_____

_____

_____

Aggressive?

_____

_____

_____

Passive-aggressive?

_____

_____

_____

Assertive?

_____

_____

_____

Name a few people in your life it's hard for you to be assertive with:

_____

_____

_____

What makes it hard to be assertive with these people?

_____

_____

_____

What situations would you like to be more assertive in?

_____

_____

_____

As you read the rest of this chapter, think about how you can use assertive language to improve your confidence and communicate your feelings and needs more effectively.

SETTING BOUNDARIES

Being assertive is about respecting others while also respecting yourself. This means that if someone's comments or behavior feel intrusive, disrespectful, or hurtful to you, you do not have to silently tolerate them. If people in your life are accustomed to you managing conflict in an aggressive, passive, or passive-aggressive manner, they might be surprised when you start approaching them assertively. At first, they might push back at your efforts to set boundaries, especially if they know that in the past, they could pester you until you'd eventually cave. If you stand firm, they'll learn that you are serious.

Be prepared to have the boundaries you set resented and denied by some, especially by people who feel entitled to be part of everyone else's business. Some people truly believe they are doing you a favor by pushing their views onto you. Whether or not someone has good intentions, you always have a right to request that they stop commenting on a certain aspect of your life.

Boundaries work best when we first use words and then reinforce them with behavior. When someone says something that bothers you, if you simply hang up the phone or walk away, they won't know what evoked your reaction. People cannot read minds. Start by directly communicating what you need. Then communicate the action you intend to take if your request is not honored.

For instance, if your mother's criticism of your weight makes you upset, you can ask her to please stop commenting on your body. This request may be enough to get her to stop. But if she continues to criticize your weight, you can add an intended action by telling her that if she continues to comment on your body, you will end the conversation and leave the room. The next time she makes a critical comment about your size, you calmly stand up and walk out of the room. Once you have set the boundary, it is up to you to uphold it. If she starts criticizing and you don't leave the room, she will learn that it's okay to continue this behavior.

Remember that boundaries are about showing yourself respect, not about "winning." Sometimes, people will not agree with your boundary, or will try to tell you that your boundary is unnecessary. It is your job to stand firm in what matters to you, even if they don't understand why. Perhaps your mom thinks she's helping you by commenting on your weight. It's not your job to convince her otherwise. If she wants to keep commenting on your body, that is her decision, but she will have to face the consequence of her behavior, which is that you will stop engaging with her. You have been clear that if she wants to have a conversation with you, she will have to respect your boundary and refrain from that topic.

It's important to set only boundaries that you are willing and able to maintain. Threatening to never talk to someone again for the rest of your life, for example, is an extreme boundary that you may not realistically be prepared to uphold.

BOUNDARIES DIALOGUE

Here are some examples of boundary-setting language. You can play around with different word choices to find statements that work best for you. Remember that the goal is to be as clear as possible about what you want or need.

"Please stop kicking the back of my seat."

"I need your help folding this laundry."

"I cannot take on this project right now. I will let you know when I have more time available."

"If you continue to call me names, I am going to hang up the phone."

"Please do not comment on my appearance."

"I am not going to discuss that topic."

NEEDS

You may have heard of Maslow's hierarchy of needs. At the most basic level are our survival needs: things like air, food, water, sleep, and going to the bathroom. In most situations, these needs must be met before we can focus on anything else. When you desperately have to go to the bathroom, it becomes difficult to think about much else for very long.

Once our basic needs have been met, we turn our attention to social and emotional needs, but not always in the order Maslow proposed. For some people, the need for love is very strong, while for others, learning and growth are bigger priorities.

In Exercise 5.7 (page 98), you will reflect on the needs that drove your addiction, the needs you've neglected, and the needs you wish to prioritize in recovery.

Maslow's Hierarchy of Needs

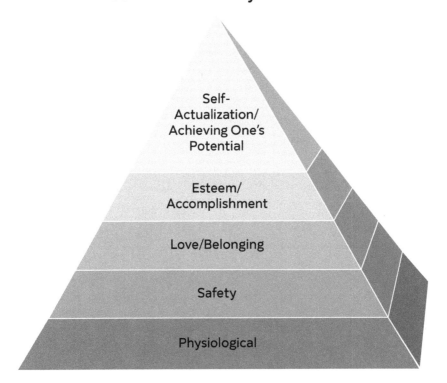

Needs List

Connection
Acceptance
Affection
Appreciation
Belonging
Cooperation
Communication
Closeness
Community
Companionship
Compassion
Consideration
Consistency
Empathy
Inclusion
Intimacy
Love
Mutuality
Nurturing
Respect/Self-Respect
Safety
Security
Shelter
Touch
Water
Independence
Trust
Warmth

Honesty
Authenticity
Integrity
Presence
Play
Joy
Humor
Peace
Beauty
Communion
Ease
Equality
Harmony
Inspiration
Order
Physical Well-Being
Air
Food
Movement/Exercise
Rest/Sleep
Sexual Expression
Understanding
Autonomy
Choice
Freedom
To Understand and
Be Understood

Meaning
Awareness
Celebration of Life
Challenge
Clarity
Competence
Consciousness
Contribution
Creativity
Discovery
Efficacy
Effectiveness
Growth
Hope
Learning
Mourning
Participation
Purpose
Self-Expression
Stimulation
To Matter
Stability
Support
To Know and Be Known
To See and Be Seen
Space
Spontaneity

EXERCISE 5.7 WHAT NEEDS DID MY ADDICTION MEET?

Use the Needs List to answer the following:

Which needs did you try to satisfy through using drugs or alcohol?

_____

_____

_____

Which did you neglect while focusing on drinking or getting high?

_____

_____

_____

Which needs are easiest for you to recognize and meet in your life today?

_____

_____

_____

Which needs are most important for you today? What (or who) helps you meet them?

_____

_____

_____

Which are hardest for you to recognize and meet?

_____

_____

_____

If a relative, friend, or partner has been negatively affected by your addiction, that relationship may take time to heal. You cannot control their feelings or be assured that they will forgive you. All you can do is offer sincere apologies and demonstrate through your daily actions that you are committed to change.

Consider getting your loved ones involved in your recovery by bringing them to a meeting, group, or individual therapy session when your treatment team allows it. This gives loved ones the chance to learn firsthand about recovery and how to support you. If you're in a relationship, you and your partner may benefit from couples therapy to address challenges related to your addiction and recovery, and to strengthen the relationship. Similarly, families often go through an adjustment phase when one member enters recovery, and family therapy can provide tools for handling this process and working through conflict.

Loved ones can also attend support groups for those affected by another's addiction, such as Al-Anon. Some of these groups are listed in the Resources section at the end of this book (page 159).

Tips and Strategies for Healthy Relationships

- Start with yourself. Use the exercises from this chapter on recognizing your strengths and building self-compassion.

- Communicate assertively. Let people know how you like to be treated, and speak up when their actions hurt you.

- Have some language in your back pocket for setting boundaries. Knowing what you'll say ahead of time will help you stand firm.

- No one is perfect. Apologize when you hurt someone, and be willing to forgive if someone genuinely regrets hurting you.

- When a friend or loved one does something you appreciate, recognize and reinforce it. Thank them or offer a genuine compliment.

- Relationships are two-way streets. Don't expect the other person to always be the one to reach out or initiate plans.

- Similarly, if you are putting in all of the effort, tell the other person how that makes you feel.

CHAPTER SIX

High-Risk Situations and Environments

Recovery is not about reaching a destination; it's about staying active in the journey. It's not as if you wake up one day fully "recovered" and then live the rest of your life unbothered by relapse triggers. Chapter 6 will help you identify high-risk situations and establish a plan for handling those situations without slipping into old behavior patterns.

Safely and Smartly Participating in Life

Unless you live in a cave, there is no way to completely avoid high-risk situations. Chances are good that eventually you will be in a situation where you are vulnerable. Much of the time it is relatively easy to avoid environments that will expose you to drugs or alcohol. If you used in a particular setting, and you are not required to be in that setting to fulfill your responsibilities as a parent, employee, student, or other important roles in your life, then it probably makes sense to avoid that setting, at least for a while. See whether it impacts your well-being at all to refrain from going to particular parties, bars, or clubs. Over time, you may find that as you develop new hobbies and engage in new activities, your lifestyle is rewarding without spending time in those old places.

In chapter 5 (page 77) you explored how relationships can help or harm your recovery. Once you recognize which relationships cause you stress, make you feel negatively about yourself, or pressure you to use, and you change how you approach those people—including setting firm boundaries—you'll be better able to build a social life that does not put you at risk of relapse.

During times that you feel strong, it is wise to capitalize on your confidence by looking out for your future self. You can help reduce your risk of relapsing by deleting phone numbers of dealers, unfollowing any accounts on social media that are triggering to you or that glamorize your drug of choice, and getting rid of all paraphernalia. It's harder to go through with these actions when stress levels are high, so many people in recovery prefer to take these steps while they are in a supportive environment, such as in the safety of their therapist's office or a support group, or while in programming at a treatment center. If you are not regularly meeting with a professional, you can enlist the help of a friend or sponsor to support you through removing these triggers from your life.

 ## EXERCISE 6.1 ENLISTING SUPPORT FOR RELAPSE PREVENTION

Going back to the people you mentioned in Exercises 5.1 (page 79) and 5.2 (page 81), consider how you can enlist them to support your relapse-prevention plan.

Who will you go to when cravings strike? If it depends on the situation, list the different situations and who will be the best support for each:

_____

_____

_____

_____

What will you need to tell these support people in advance? Write a sentence or two using assertive "I" statements to make your requests. For example, "I need to be able to call someone when I'm feeling the urge to have a drink. When I have urges, I need you to remind me of why I'm in recovery and distract me for a few minutes. Can I count on you for this?"

_____

_____

_____

_____

If there is someone you'd like to ask for support, but you are hesitant, what is getting in the way of asking them?

_____

_____

What would it take for you to be willing to ask them?

_____

_____

It is wise to have this conversation with multiple people. The worst-case scenario is that they say no and you move on to finding someone else to serve in this role. You also need more than one person to agree to support you because you shouldn't rely on a single person to be available 24/7. Remember too that the members of your treatment team, including your therapist and/or sponsor, are also committed to helping you stay in recovery. If you ask them, they are usually willing to take a phone call or answer an e-mail or text message from you when you're struggling.

If you don't have a treatment team, then it is wise to retain some phone numbers for hotlines in the event that your friends or family aren't available in a time of need. Some hotlines are listed in the Resources section at the end of this workbook.

Some people manage to avoid parties and outings where alcohol or drugs will be present, without it taking a toll on their social lives. However, for better or worse, the use of alcohol and other drugs is embedded in cultures and communities all over the world. Sometimes completely avoiding these events and activities can feel isolating. Everyone is different, so there is no one-size-fits-all plan for safely engaging in these situations. This chapter will provide some ideas on how to handle situations that commonly put people in recovery at risk of relapse. Take these ideas and tailor them to fit your life.

EXERCISE 6.2 BEING PREPARED FOR LIFE ACTIVITIES

I've assembled here some of the common life activities that could pop up over the course of your recovery. For each one, consider how risky it feels to you today. Rate on a scale of 0 (absolutely no risk of relapse) to 10 (completely certain that I will use). Recognize that you are basing your ratings on what you know about yourself, including how you typically act and feel in a given situation.

0	**1**	**2**	**3**	**4**	**5**	**6**	**7**	**8**	**9**	**10**
absolutely no risk of relapse	extremely safe situation, highly unlikely to relapse	very unlikely to relapse	somewhat unlikely to relapse	unlikely to relapse	could go either way, 50/50 chance of relapse	could relapse, but not very likely	somewhat likely to relapse	very likely to relapse	extremely likely to relapse, lots of risks involved	completely certain I will relapse

While celebrating the holidays with family _____

During or after a fight with my significant other _____

At an office holiday party, networking event, or work-related happy hour _____

Out with friends on New Year's Eve _____

After receiving a promotion _____

After being criticized at work _____

At a wedding _____

Watching a movie or TV show where the characters are using _____

Hanging out with a friend who still uses (name the friends this applies to) _____

Most of these experiences will likely happen at some point—many of them more than once—so it's important to be proactive with your relapse-prevention plan. When these events actually happen, pay attention to how they feel for you—do they elicit urges that are as strong as you rated in this activity?

LEARNING TO HALT

Now that you've evaluated the types of situations that increase your risk of relapsing, it's time to talk strategy. Research shows that the majority of relapses occur during the first six months of recovery, so it is important to establish your action plan from the beginning.

Notice whether the activities you rated highest in Exercise 6.2 (page 104) had anything in common. Perhaps they all elicit an intense emotion, involve interpersonal conflicts, or relate to major life changes. For some people, being surprised by critical feedback from a boss is harder to handle than receiving it in an expected situation, like in a quarterly review. Everyone's triggers are different; as you get to know which situations make you most vulnerable, you'll feel less surprised or overwhelmed when some urges are more intense than others.

Being either emotionally depleted or activated in some way makes it harder to control impulses. HALT is a good acronym to help you remember this. When you are *hungry*, *angry*, *lonely*, or *tired*, you are more likely to make impulsive decisions. Obviously, feeling hungry, angry, lonely, and tired are normal parts of daily life, so it's vital to be sure you're taking care of yourself physically and emotionally to avoid relapsing from HALT.

Intense positive emotions, such as pleasure or joy, can also increase our risk of making impulsive decisions. If you know this happens to you, have a plan in place so you don't sabotage your recovery. If you see drugs or alcohol as "rewards" or associate them with celebrating, you will need to learn to enjoy your positive feelings in new ways.

RED FLAGS THAT YOU'RE AT RISK OF RELAPSE

Learning to spot risk factors can alert you to times you need extra help or support. Behavior patterns that often indicate a person is at risk of relapsing include:

- Engaging obsessively in a "replacement" addiction, such as eating, gambling, shopping, video games, or pornography

- Spending time in places where you used to buy or use drugs or alcohol

- Keeping drugs or alcohol in your home

- Regularly hanging out with people who are using

- Isolating yourself or withdrawing from friends and recovery supports

- Skipping therapy appointments or blowing off meetings and support groups

- Noticing any sudden changes in your energy level, appetite, sleep, and activity level

If you notice yourself falling into any of these patterns, please seek support immediately. Refer to the Resources section at the end of this book (page 159) if you need a hotline to call or a directory for finding treatment.

EXERCISE 6.3 DECIDING WHICH SITUATIONS NEED RELAPSE-PREVENTION PLANS

For the following areas of your life, identify situations that you'd rate at a 5 or above on the scale in Exercise 6.2 (page 104). Once you've identified these situations, the information in the next section will help you come up with an action plan for handling each situation.

Situations at work:

_____

_____

People in your work environment:

_____

_____

Situations at home:

_____

_____

People in your home environment:

_____

_____

Social situations:

_____

_____

Friends or acquaintances in your social circle:

_____

_____

(Continued)

Family situations:

_____

_____

Issues with particular family members:

_____

_____

Holidays, birthdays, anniversaries (including anniversaries of things like traumatic events or a death), seasons, or times of the year that can be risky:

_____

_____

Awareness is your best defense. Simply knowing how these situations can impact you can help you stay cautious about them. There are two intelligent responses to these situations: (1) Avoid them, if it is possible to do so without harming your quality of life, or (2) Create a solid relapse-prevention plan and proceed with caution.

CREATING A PERSONALIZED ACTION PLAN

Exercise 6.3 (page 107) helped you identify the situations that pose the highest risk of relapse. If you still choose to enter these situations, it's important to do so only with proper support and a plan in place. Getting overly confident and dismissing the possibility of relapse can actually increase your risk of relapsing. It's better to assume you need the plan than to discover you needed it once it's too late.

If you know or suspect that drugs and alcohol will be present where you are going, decide ahead of time what you will say or do to refuse them if they are offered to you. Ask a friend or therapist to role-play with you—they pretend to offer you a drink or drug, and you practice saying "no thanks." Take a cue from actors, who practice their lines so much that they can speak them automatically even in the face of stage fright; rehearsing your lines will help you say them as planned even in the heat of the moment.

Having a built-in escape plan in most situations can help you stay safe in the face of tough emotions, conflicts, social pressure, or other relapse triggers. An escape plan can be as simple as knowing where the restroom is when you're out at a restaurant or at a friend's house, in the event that you need to step away from the group for a few minutes, and keeping your cell phone with you in case you need to call or text someone for support. You can also set yourself up ahead of time when going to an event where others will be getting intoxicated by offering to be their designated driver. The responsibilities of getting your passengers home safely and staying out of legal trouble can be powerful motivators to help you stay sober for the night.

Aside from having an escape plan, you should also be familiar with some basic skills that can help you overcome in-the-moment urges. Think about what you can do to distract yourself. Plan to focus on anything else—whether a mental game (like trying to name a food that starts with each letter of the alphabet, or counting the ceiling tiles), or a distracting activity, like cleaning, going for a walk, or listening to a podcast. The research shows that cravings typically peak around 20 to 30 minutes—and then they subside. If you can distract yourself for long enough, eventually the urge will pass.

A technique called "urge surfing" is one way to mindfully engage in the experience of your urges while watching them pass. It involves noticing the sensations in your body that arise when you're having urges, watching them rise in intensity, build up to their peak, and then crash and subside. Your urges are like ocean waves—they build up more and more until they are at their strongest, and then they break at their peak and subside. If you can allow your urges to reach their peak without using behaviors, you will find that they always subside. If you fight with the urge, try to make it go away, or turn to another behavior (like self-harm), you actually end up making the urge stick around longer, and you may even transfer your addiction to something new. With practice, you can get good at riding out your urges much as you would surf a wave.

Another useful tool to have at your disposal is called "opposite action." This is a technique from dialectical behavior therapy (DBT) whereby you do the opposite of what you have the urge to do. If you feel depressed and have the urge to isolate, the opposite action would be to reach out to other people. If you have the urge to attack someone, the opposite action could be to walk away or be nice to them. If you have the urge to harm yourself, the opposite action would be any act of self-love, like taking a bath or wrapping up in a cozy blanket. The goal is not to make feelings or urges go away, but to set in motion an action that is helpful to your recovery and not harmful. When you act in harmful ways, the feelings get worse, and then you have to deal with the consequences of your harmful actions.

If you have an escape plan, familiar practiced language for refusing alcohol and drugs, and tried-and-true skills for distracting and calming yourself when urges strike, you have all of the tools needed for protecting yourself in the face of relapse triggers. Now that you have identified your risks and gotten suggestions for how to cope, Exercise 6.4 will help you put it all together, selecting the tools and strategies that appeal most to you and putting them into a concrete action plan.

 ## EXERCISE 6.4 PART 1: MY ACTION PLAN FOR HIGH-RISK SITUATIONS

Answer the following questions to create your personalized action plan.

What strategies and tools have you used in the past to successfully ride out a craving to use?

_____

_____

_____

_____

When cravings show up, what are three things you can do to *distract* yourself while you wait for them to pass?

_____

_____

_____

Imagine that you are in a situation where other people are using, like at a party. What will you say if someone offers you drugs or alcohol?

_____

_____

_____

Imagine that you decide to relapse. What are some potential negative consequences that would result? List all possible ways this relapse could impact you:

_____

_____

_____

Now list all of the ways you have benefited from sobriety. How have you grown? How has your life become more satisfying since you stopped using?

_____

_____

_____

Refer to this exercise often, especially when you are expecting to enter a situation you identified as risky. Every time you successfully ride out a craving, pay attention to what helped you do so and record your success. Over time, you will learn which tools are most helpful in each situation.

◢◣◢ EXERCISE 6.4 PART 2: MY ESCAPE PLAN FOR HIGH-RISK SITUATIONS

Now you'll create an exit strategy for the high-risk situations you identified in Exercise 6.3 (page 107). List these situations here and write what you can do to escape each one.

Work-related situations:

_____

_____

List three places you could go (such as to the bathroom, to a nearby coffee shop, for a walk around the block):

_____

_____

_____

Situations at home:

_____

_____

List three places you could go:

_____

_____

_____

Social situations:

_____

_____

List three places you could go:

_____

_____

_____

Family situations:

_____

_____

List three places you could go:

_____

_____

_____

Holidays and celebrations:

_____

_____

List three places you could go:

_____

_____

_____

Other:

_____

_____

List three places you could go:

_____

_____

_____

Before you enter these or any other potentially risky situations, do this exercise and identify some places you can escape to, even for just a few minutes, to collect yourself. It is not always possible to completely leave a situation, but stepping away to the restroom, going to your bedroom and closing the door, or stepping out of your office to make a quick phone call to one of your support people can help you handle the situation without relapsing.

Staying Alert to Relapse Potential

Awareness is the best defense against relapse. In this chapter, you've explored various types of thoughts, feelings, and behaviors that indicate you are vulnerable to relapsing. You have a detailed action plan for relapse prevention that you can take everywhere with you. No plan is completely foolproof, though. It's important to watch for signs that you need professional support.

If you find that over a period of time your urges get more frequent or more overwhelming, you may need to seek a higher level of support than what you currently have. Similarly, if you find that you're inadvertently channeling your urges into using something else that could become obsessive or detrimental, like food, exercise, sex, self-harm, or video games, this is an indication that you have transferred your addiction and should seek professional help. It could be you have not fully addressed the underlying issues that contribute to addictive behaviors.

Certain thought patterns also indicate that you could use more support. Constantly thinking about using drugs or alcohol, or believing you could get away with using just one time, are thoughts to watch for and seek support if they persist. If you find yourself setting unrealistic and impossible goals, being hard on yourself, and trying to avoid your problems, you may be setting yourself up for a relapse. It is wise to seek professional help.

Remember that recovery is not linear. It is natural to feel confident and solid for some time, and then start struggling again from time to time. This does not mean you have taken steps backward. It actually shows intelligence to know when you are struggling and acknowledge that you need more help. If you do this, you will get back on track much more quickly than if you shame yourself or go into denial.

STEPPING UP SUPPORT

Stepping up your support may mean increasing the time you spend with members of your treatment team or adding more recovery-focused activities to your daily routine. It could mean starting to see a therapist or joining a support group if you don't already do those things. Or, if you already see a therapist or attend a group, you may increase the frequency of your sessions, such as going from once per week to twice per week while you are in a period of crisis or feeling particularly challenged by urges. If you've been decreasing your support for some time, such as tapering down to meeting every other week with your therapist, you can always ask to go back to more frequent meetings until you feel ready to step down again.

If you are in an outpatient program, you may consider stepping up to a more intensive program or enrolling in a residential program if you are able to do so. Even if you have already completed a higher level of treatment, you may benefit from another stint in a residential program. This can be especially helpful following a relapse. Often you will gain new insights the second time around that you hadn't been ready for previously, and a refresher course in the tools and coping skills will help make them more habitual.

ENSURING THE RIGHT SUPPORT FOR YOU

In some cases, the problem is not the amount of support you're getting, but the type of support. Treatment is not one-size-fits-all, so you'll have to reflect on what works and what doesn't work for you.

If you're in therapy, ask yourself:

- Do you have a strong relationship with your therapist?

- Are you remembering the things you've learned in your sessions?

- Is your therapist providing the amount of structure, guidance, or support you need?

Some people prefer a therapist who teaches concrete tools and skills, while others prefer nondirective questions and comments that allow them to foster insight on their own. If you are feeling stuck in therapy, consider discussing this in your next session. Therapists have different specialties and use different approaches depending on their training, education, and experience, so not every client will be a perfect match for their brand of therapy. Ask your therapist if he or she thinks you could benefit from a different style or approach than what they've been using, and see if you can troubleshoot together. If you simply find that your therapist rubs you the wrong way or you don't feel comfortable with them, see whether you can find someone who is a better fit for you.

If you attend 12-step meetings, consider whether you feel adequately supported and understood by your peers. Some people go to several different meetings before they discover their "home base." While some 12-step meetings are attended by a broad range of people, others might cater to a specific population. For instance, some meetings cater to military veterans, and this shared identity helps members relate to one another's experiences more easily. You may find that you relate best to peers who share your gender, age range, or cultural background, and it's fine to seek these out. It is also helpful to find a meeting that matches your own spiritual identity. Some meetings promote themselves as more religious in nature, while others are nondenominational or agnostic. If you feel out of place, consider what aspects of a group would make you feel more like you fit in.

Strategies for When High-Risk Situations and Environments Make You Crave

- Turn to your support system. When cravings strike, call a friend, sponsor, family member, or therapist to help you manage urges and keep you accountable.

- Don't try to ignore or brush off daily hassles. The stress and problems you encounter every day can build up over time and lead to intense cravings when you reach your limit. Use healthy emotion regulation, vent and process through your stress, and write about it in a journal to make sure you are letting steam out in little ways every day.

- Escape the situation if necessary. Leaving the room, even for just a few minutes, gives you a chance to collect yourself and calm down. If it's realistic, you may also want to leave the situation completely to keep yourself from relapsing.

- When the consequences of escaping a situation outweigh the benefits, take a mental break from the environment. Close your eyes, breathe deeply, and imagine that you are in a safe and comfortable environment.

- Practice skills for riding out the urges. Try some of the techniques from this workbook, like urge surfing, focusing on the sights, sounds, and colors of the room, focusing on sensations in your body, or distracting yourself until the urge subsides.

- Use any or all of the coping strategies you listed in Exercise 6.4 (page 110) on your relapse-prevention plan.

- Think about what it would be like to eliminate this high-risk environment from your life. Make a list of pros (benefits of staying in the environment) and cons (the risks if you stay).

PART THREE

Preventing Relapse Every Day

Now that you've developed new strategies for handling the challenges of daily life, you are ready to put what you've learned into practice. This part of the workbook will help you to establish new routines and rituals that do not involve substance abuse, and to redefine your personal identity by connecting to what matters most to you. It will guide you through the process of recognizing your values and living a meaningful, satisfying life.

CHAPTER SEVEN

Lifestyle Change

You have worked hard to prepare yourself for the journey of recovery. In your suitcase, you now carry the knowledge, tools, and skills you've learned throughout this book. The exercises have helped you create your road map. As you move along, you don't need a fancy GPS system to guide you. All you need is a simple compass. Chapter 7 will teach you to recognize your values and make healthy lifestyle changes that allow you to read your internal compass. Your true north is where you go when you are proud of who you are, when you are living a life of purpose.

Supporting Change

There's a common misconception that a "good life" is one that constantly gets better. Maybe you recognize that life has ups and downs, but secretly hope there will come a time when there are only ups, where life just gets better over time, all the way to the end. Many humans seem to believe this (though they may not realize it), constantly striving to achieve the next goal and rack up the next accomplishment, treating any hardship as simply a setback on their path to the top.

Reality check: Life doesn't work like that. You probably know this logically, but on an emotional level this is hard to accept. The idea that life *should* be getting better and better gives us that illusion of control, by telling us that if we work hard enough, we can reach a place in life where unwanted situations never happen to us.

A more helpful (and realistic) way to approach life is to look at where you focus your energy. A good life is not one that constantly gets better and better, but rather, one full of meaning and purpose. When you recognize what matters to you, and you devote your energy to those priorities, you open yourself up to the full experience of being alive. You allow the parts of life you cannot control, like thoughts, feelings, and other people's behaviors, to simply happen without wasting energy trying to control them, and you see more clearly what you do have control over. Taking this approach to life will aid your recovery by freeing up your energy to focus on what fulfills you.

VALUES

An important element of this more realistic and rewarding approach to life is recognizing your values. Your values are the qualities, characteristics, and principles that are important to you. No one else can tell you what your values are; they are uniquely yours to choose. Digging deep to examine what matters most to you can be quite powerful. Many people find that for much of their lives, they've been trying to adhere to a set of values given to them by others, such as what they were taught in their family, school, or culture. While some of these values may truly align with what matters to you, it is also possible that some of them don't completely resonate for the life you wish to lead. Alternatively, you might hold some of these values, but find that other values are more important to you. Exercise 7.1 (page 122) will help you identify these.

Tolerance	Happiness	Prestige	Nature
Learning	Beauty	Power	Accuracy
Family	Peace	Variety	Spirituality
Financial security	Self-control	Leisure	Religion
Balance	Artistic expression	Organization	Love

Security	Courage	Generosity	Independence
Flexibility	Integrity	Achievement	Cooperation
Kindness	Fun	Health	Efficiency
Creativity	Competition	Physical fitness	Perseverance
Friendship	Authenticity	Challenge	Wisdom
Forgiveness	Tradition	Leadership	
Humor	Hope	Recognition	
Adventure	Fairness	Loyalty	

 ## EXERCISE 7.1 IDENTIFYING CORE VALUES

This exercise will help you home in on your most important values, so that you know where to focus your energy going forward.

What sort of person do you want to be? How would you want others to describe you?

_____

_____

What principles do you want to stand for?

_____

_____

What do you think the world needs more of to become a better place?

_____

_____

Using the list of examples, along with any other values that come to mind, list your top five values. You're not carving these in stone—your values can change over the course of your life—just try to focus on who you want to be *today*. And you don't have to list them in order of importance, as they could be equally important to you.

_____

_____

_____

_____

_____

You've identified your values, the qualities most important to you in life. These are the things you will want to prioritize. When you live in line with your values, you feel good about yourself and the type of person you are. When you neglect your values, you tend to feel negatively about yourself and your life. In Exercise 7.2, you'll explore the ways of living that align with your values and help you connect with the life you are meant to live.

 ## EXERCISE 7.2 LIVING OUT YOUR VALUES IN DAILY LIFE

List some behaviors that demonstrate each of your five values in action. These behaviors should be concrete, specific, and measurable. For example, if you value *family*, you might list behaviors such as:

- Playing with my children every day, and asking about their day when I see them in the evening

- Doing an activity we enjoy together or having one-on-one quality time with my wife at least once per week

- Spending holidays with family

- Tell my family members "I love you" whenever we say goodbye

(Continued)

What are some behaviors that reflect each of your values?

Value: _____

Behaviors:

_____

_____

_____

Value: _____

Behaviors:

_____

_____

_____

Value: _____

Behaviors:

_____

_____

_____

Value: _____

Behaviors:

_____

_____

_____

Value: _____

Behaviors:

_____

_____

_____

The mantra here is "progress, not perfection." No one lives out values perfectly on a daily basis. Sometimes one value takes priority over the others. Using these behaviors as guidelines can help you see what matters to you and set realistic goals to focus on.

WHEN ADDICTION TOOK OVER

When using behaviors were a regular part of your life, they likely took priority over the things you actually value. Consider Tracy's story:

Tracy always hated being lied to, and she felt guilty when she lied. She didn't like how it felt when she told someone what she thought they wanted to hear, instead of telling the truth. When Tracy got to high school, her friends started smoking pot, and she occasionally joined in. One day, when she was 16, Tracy was mugged at gunpoint on her way home from school, and the experience plagued her daily. She had nightmares, flashbacks, and became nervous to go places alone. To cope, she started smoking pot multiple times per day. At school and at home, she did all she could to mask the fact that she was high all of the time.

Over the years, Tracy's habit continued. In her early 20s, she got a job that required random drug testing, so she bought synthetic urine off the Internet and used it to pass the tests. Her self-esteem was tanked, but she couldn't recognize why. Finally, at age 25, she began to see a therapist, who helped her understand how the traumatic event led to her heavy marijuana use. She also realized that she felt like an "awful person" because she valued honesty, so the dishonest behaviors she had developed—like pretending she was sober and faking her drug tests—went against a very important value for her.

As she learned other ways to deal with her emotions and started to let go of drugs, Tracy noticed she no longer felt guilty and guarded all of the time. She could pass drug tests without lying; she could show up to family functions confident that she wasn't acting high. She was finally living honestly, and, as a result, she felt increasingly satisfied with how she was showing up in her job, social life, and relationships.

When things feel "off" in life, we often go looking for the solution in ways that cause us more difficulty. Instead, it can help to look at our core values, and recognize whether we have been neglecting any of them. Often, the reason things feel "off" is that we aren't giving enough attention to the things that matter most to us, and seeing what needs attention can help us get back on track. Exercise 7.3 (page 126) will help you identify those important things.

EXERCISE 7.3 **WHAT NEEDS YOUR ATTENTION?**

Of your top five values, which ones suffered most in your addiction?

_____

_____

_____

Which values would you like to focus on in recovery?

_____

_____

What behaviors from Exercise 7.2 (page 123) are you willing to commit to:

This week?

_____

_____

This month?

_____

_____

This year?

_____

_____

The behaviors you've identified can be used as _goals_ for your short-, mid-, and long-term future. Write these goals somewhere accessible, and check in with yourself regularly to evaluate how you're doing. Notice how focusing on these goals makes you feel about yourself and the life you're leading.

Living a Balanced Life

To pursue the things that matter most to you, it is important to have a strong foundation. Self-care gives you this foundation, and it involves meeting those needs you explored in chapter 5 (page 77). While it might seem obvious, many people are surprised to see how their stress is directly related to things like lack of sleep, poor nutrition, or physical inactivity. Creating healthy lifestyle habits in these basic areas can do wonders for building your resilience in recovery.

EXERCISE

Our bodies were meant to move. Research consistently shows that physical activity has physical and emotional benefits that help with sobriety. Not only does exercise stimulate the release of endorphins and other feel-good chemicals in the brain, but it also can provide an energy boost, improve circulation, and improve the quality and regulation of your sleep.

Exercise does not have to follow a strict regimen, and all bodies are different in what they need. The goal is to find ways you enjoy moving your body, and do them as often as you like, without creating rules or beating yourself up when something else takes priority above exercise. Look for ways to move your body that make you feel strong, empowered, and appreciative of what your body is capable of. For some, the reward of building a skill, technique, and coordination draws them to activities like soccer, basketball, or dance. Others find it therapeutic to release aggression through boxing or going for a run. You may enjoy the flexibility and mental release of practicing yoga. Perhaps you enjoy being outdoors, and rock climbing, hiking, or going for a walk through nature makes you feel recharged.

Exercise and fitness do not have to be financially taxing, either. If joining a gym or fitness studio is unrealistic, there are plenty of other options. Go to the library to read about how to do a new activity, or go online to find video tutorials and workout routines. Plenty of sports leagues are free or low-cost, and if you live near a park, you may run into people playing pickup basketball or other sports you can join in. Visit your local YMCA or other community center and see what's available. Download a fitness app on your smartphone and follow along with the routines. Once you've discovered a variety of activities that bring you joy, you'll be able to tell which one your body is craving at a given time. Remember that sometimes your body needs rest, so don't force yourself to exercise when you are tired, injured, or have pressing work commitments that require you to forgo exercise until you've met a deadline.

NUTRITION

Research shows that eating a variety of foods and nutrients not only gives us enough energy to move through daily activities, but also affects our mental health. The human brain needs sufficient nutrients to fuel things like memory, attention, concentration, creativity, and learning. A healthy diet means consuming as many fresh, whole foods as possible in a variety of colors, flavors, and textures, with a balance of protein, complex carbohydrates, and healthy fats.

It is typically more productive to listen to your body's cues for hunger, fullness, and satisfaction than it is to obsess over food or try to eat "perfectly." Everyone's needs are different, so there is no one-size-fits-all meal plan, despite what some diet companies will tell you. Learning a bit about which foods contain various vitamins, minerals, and other nutrients can help you recognize whether you're getting a good balance.

Take note of how you feel after you eat certain foods; this will help you discover what a satisfying, balanced diet is for you. For instance, if you feel hungry very shortly after breakfast, you can explore whether you simply aren't eating enough food at breakfast, or whether you are lacking variety in the nutrients you're eating. You may have to do some trial and error to discover what happens when you add more protein, carbs, or fats to a meal and how what you eat influences your energy and alertness throughout the day.

Overall, pay attention to your relationship with food and recognize whether you reach for certain foods when you're not physically hungry. In these cases, you may be using food to try to satisfy an emotional need, such as loneliness, stress, or boredom. While it is only human to try to "solve" emotions through various behaviors (and you know this very well as someone in recovery), it is not typically effective in the long run.

If you're interested in learning more about the specifics and better understanding what your body needs, you may wish to consult a nutrition professional, such as a registered dietitian.

SLEEP

Sleep is connected to all sorts of physical and mental health factors. Your brain and body need sleep to store information you have learned in your memory, repair your organs and other functional systems, and balance your hormones and blood sugar. Research has shown that sleep deprivation has a negative impact on social skills, decision-making, problem solving, creativity, attention, and mood, among other health risks.

When it comes to recovery, sleep is a vital piece of the puzzle. When you are sleep deprived, you are more prone to feeling irritable, critical of yourself and others, and impulsive. You may have a harder time controlling your behavior, so you may make a decision you later regret, such as relapsing. Generally, most people need between seven and nine hours of sleep per night to feel sufficiently rested the next day, but everyone is different. Do your best to make sleep a priority and to get the amount that allows you to function well each day.

TIPS FOR IMPROVING SLEEP QUALITY

- Eliminate light in the bedroom, especially light from TV or electronics. If outside light bothers you, close your blinds, use blackout shades, or wear an eyeshade.

- Eliminate sound if it bothers you. Wear earplugs if necessary, or if you find background noise soothing, use a white noise machine, fan, or app on your phone to provide ambient sound.

- Limit your use of screens in the two hours before bed.

- Stay nourished and hydrated throughout the day so you don't find yourself eating a big meal or drinking a lot of liquids right before bed, which can wake you for repeated bathroom visits during the night.

- Exercise regularly, and pay attention to how it affects your sleep. Exercise can help you sleep better, but some people find that exercising too late in the day keeps them awake at night, so plan accordingly.

- Don't drink caffeine in the afternoon. For some, this means no caffeine after 2:00 p.m., while others find they must stop much earlier in the day.

- Optimize the comfort of your sleep environment. Improve the air quality and circulation with a fan or humidifier or by opening a window. For some people, it is tough to sleep when the room is too hot.

- Invest in the most comfortable mattress, blankets, sheets, and pillow that you can afford.

- Establish a relaxing bedtime ritual. This can involve sipping chamomile tea, taking a warm bath or shower, lighting a scented candle or using lavender essential oil, or following a guided relaxation such as a meditation or yoga for sleep.

- If you find repetitive thoughts and worries keep you awake, try writing in a journal before bed. Sometimes the simple act of getting it down on paper can help your mind let it go for the night.

SUPPORT SYSTEM

In chapter 5 (page 77), you explored the various ways that relationships support a successful recovery. Research has shown that social support might be just as important as nutritious food and exercise when it comes to a person's health. In communities with lots of social support, people typically live longer and have fewer health problems than in communities characterized by isolation and competitiveness. Often, when people are busy and stressed, social life is the first thing to go. This is unfortunate, given the many benefits of a support system of people you can rely on for encouragement, empathy, and rejuvenation.

If you think of your relationships as chores to be completed or tasks to check off a never-ending to-do list, you defeat the purpose of having them in the first place. Relationships are meant to fill you up, not drain you. If you find that you feel stressed or overwhelmed by social plans, see if you can find the source of those feelings. It is possible that you've formed a negative association with socializing, especially if you were taught growing up that you were obligated to spend time with certain people against your will. While it could be that the people you are spending time with are not ones you truly want to be around, your brain could be telling you a story about how you "should" be spending your time and energy. Think about whether these explanations might apply. Do you genuinely enjoy the company of the people you're spending time with? Do you feel distracted by other things going on in your life? Are there other activities you'd prefer to be doing with these friends or loved ones? Are you craving some alone time, but pushing yourself to be social? Take an honest look at what you need from your social supports; this will help you see where to make changes.

R&R

Humans are not machines. We can't be productive every moment of every day without eventually crashing. When it comes to your overall health, taking time to recharge and relax is just as important as the time you spend doing activities. Oftentimes in Western culture, people wear being "busy" as a badge of honor, but the reality is that we choose what keeps us busy. Allowing yourself to do nothing from time to time takes self-compassion and awareness of your limits. If you push yourself to stay busy all of the time, you are sure to burn out. Give yourself permission to take breaks from the hustle and bustle, whether you prefer to take a nap, watch a mindless TV show, lounge around in your pajamas after a busy week, or lay outside in the sunshine on a day off from work. When you schedule time for "R&R," you can come back to the activities of your daily life feeling energized and refreshed.

DO WHAT YOU LOVE

There's a truism: Life is too short to waste on things that don't make you happy. When you focus your energy on the things you care about, you experience life in a much richer and fuller way than when you focus on things that bother you. While you know by now that you cannot control what thoughts and feelings pop up, or what others say or do, or what happens in the future, you are certainly in charge of your daily actions. Make it a point to behave in ways that align with your values, and pursue what you care about the most. This is the kindest thing you can do, not only for yourself, but also for everyone whose path you will cross in life. When you do what gives your life meaning and purpose, you put that energy out into the world to benefit others.

While some people are clearly excited by certain activities or topics, not everyone has an obvious passion they can pursue. It is more likely that you have a few different areas of life or interests that make you excited and bring you joy. Once you know what brings you joy, you can be intentional about incorporating more of it in your daily life.

If you're unsure what brings you joy, it's time to start reflecting. Think about some of your favorite memories, times when you had a lot of fun without the presence of drugs or alcohol. What were you doing? Where were you, and who were you with? What made that memory so joyful? If it was something special, like a trip or vacation, consider which elements made it so wonderful. (You'll have a chance to apply this knowledge in Exercise 7.4 [page 133].) You may have enjoyed getting to explore new places and see other cultures, trying new foods, having adventures, the tranquility of being out in nature, or the chance to slow down and relax. It is not always realistic to travel or take vacations as often as you wish, but exploration, adventure, relaxation, and learning can take place no matter where you are. If you know what you liked about these experiences, you can recognize how to do more things that bring you joy in daily life.

EXERCISE 7.4 WHAT BRINGS YOU JOY?

Recovery gets easier when you fill up your life with things that bring you joy. Fill in the blanks to brainstorm some activities and interests that appeal to you and that can enrich your daily life.

Something active I enjoy doing is:

_____

Something active I'd like to start doing is:

_____

A craft or hobby I enjoy is:

_____

A craft or hobby I'd like to try is:

_____

A new skill I'd like to develop is:

_____

My favorite games include:

_____

If I could play any instrument, I'd want to play:

_____

If I could learn any language, I'd like to learn:

_____

A concert, play, or live performance I'd love to see is:

_____

A trip I'd love to take is:

_____

(Continued)

Place a star beside the activities that you're most curious about, and plan to pursue those first. If you're curious about a concert, trip, or event, see what it would take to get there and set some long-term goals to work toward. Perhaps this is the push you need to start saving up for that trip you've been dying to take or that band you've always dreamed of seeing in concert.

ACTIVITIES THAT BRING JOY

Here are some pursuits and pastimes that bring many people joy. See if any of these have potential to bring you positive feelings, or if reading this list inspires you to come up with your own enjoyable activities.

- Enjoying a meal with close friends
- Cooking or baking
- Exploring new restaurants, coffee shops, boutiques, or neighborhoods
- Having a picnic in the park
- Hiking, horseback riding, swimming, canoeing, or any other outdoor activity
- Spending time in nature
- Drawing, painting, knitting, pottery, or other types of arts and crafts
- Cuddling up by the fireplace with a mug of hot cocoa in the winter
- Singing at the top of your lungs in the shower (or at a karaoke party)
- Dancing around the house in your underwear

- Teaching someone else how to do something new
- Playing with puppies or other animals
- Playing a sport or game you enjoy
- Volunteering
- Listening to music from an artist you find talented
- Listening to a comedian you enjoy or reading a comedic story or book
- Creating: writing, playing an instrument, or designing something
- Looking at artwork you find very beautiful
- Going to the beach
- Spending time with people who make you smile

Tips and Strategies for Self-Care and Health

- Be as proactive about your healthcare as your finances allow. Prioritize preventive care, and seek treatment before symptoms worsen and potentially become more expensive or life-threatening.

- Everyone gets injured or sick at some point. Don't be stubborn or go into denial when this happens to you. Go to the doctor or seek other professional care. The Internet and your well-intentioned friend are not substitutes for professional evaluation.

- Check in with yourself weekly to ensure you are meeting the basic needs discussed in this chapter, including sleep, nutrition, exercise, socialization, and relaxation. If you are neglecting one of these areas, figure out how you will address it.

- Recognize your limits. It's okay to say no to requests and invitations when you are feeling stretched thin. Pushing yourself to be social or take on another project when you're already depleted will only lead to resentment and poor performance.

- Remember to HALT—that is, to see if you feel *hungry, angry, lonely,* or *tired*. Practice recognizing these and responding in a self-compassionate way, by nourishing yourself, expressing anger in a healthy way, reaching out to social supports, or carving out time to recharge.

CHAPTER EIGHT

Preventing Relapse Every Day

The ebbs and flows of your recovery are not always predictable. You might go several weeks or months without urges, and then suddenly struggle again. Being flexible and not getting too comfortable (that is, not feeling like "That's it, I'm fully recovered, home free!") will help you meet yourself wherever you are each day. Chapter 8 will help you settle into your ongoing recovery lifestyle and learn from lapses and relapses, so you can forgive yourself and get back on track.

A Successful Recovery

Webster's dictionary defines *success* as "a favorable or desired outcome; also, the attainment of wealth, favor, or eminence." When it comes to recovery, it makes sense that the desired outcome involves a rewarding life without the problems caused by drugs or alcohol. However, since a rewarding life looks different from person to person, each of us has to define individually what successful recovery really means.

In chapter 7 (page 120), you identified and explored your personal values, which serve as the routes on your road map to a meaningful life. To define success in recovery, you have to look at how staying sober is essential for living out those values. For instance, if you value *family*, then a successful recovery is one that allows you to spend time with family, meet your responsibilities as a parent and partner, and provide a healthy and stable home environment for your loved ones. It also involves staying sober so that you can maintain the trust of your family members and be fully present at family functions.

There is no single right way to recover; there is only the way that is right for you. Exercise 8.1 will help you define your successful recovery, using your values as guides along the journey.

 ## EXERCISE 8.1 DEFINING SUCCESS FOR YOU

Remember that values are not endpoints that can be "achieved," but rather, qualities and characteristics to embody on a daily basis. Write how each of the values you identified in Exercise 7.1 (page 122) relates to your personal version of successful recovery. The first is done as an example.

Value: *Family*

How recovery supports this value: *Staying sober means I am fully present with my kids. When I have some extra money, I don't go use it on alcohol or drugs; I use it on fun family activities, clothes, toys, or books. I have a clear mind and remember to pick my kids up from school. I show up when my family needs me, and I don't lie to them.*

Value:

_____

How recovery supports this value:

_____

_____

_____

(Continued)

Value:

_____

How recovery supports this value:

_____

_____

_____

Value:

_____

How recovery supports this value:

_____

_____

_____

Value:

_____

How recovery supports this value:

_____

_____

_____

Value:

_____

How recovery supports this value:

_____

_____

_____

What you've written here sums up your definition of success in recovery. Use what you've written here to remind yourself of how you measure success and keep yourself on track.

In chapter 6 (page 101), you created a relapse-prevention plan for high-risk situations. While those situations may require extra care to prevent relapse, you'll also need to practice relapse-prevention strategies in your everyday life, even when not in high-risk situations.

When you go to the grocery store without a grocery list, you often end up buying items you didn't really need or forgetting items you meant to buy. Similarly, when you go through daily activities on autopilot, without a plan, you risk doing something you didn't intend to do. Staying aware of the values you explored in Exercise 8.1 (page 137) will help you lead a pro-recovery life. Keep these values and the actions they inspire at the forefront of your mind daily, as a sort of daily "grocery list" for relapse prevention.

Your values drive your actions, so build a life around those values and find other people who share them so that they can influence you in a positive way. While of course you cannot completely eliminate all reminders of drugs, alcohol, and the lifestyle you once had, you can certainly build a "bubble" of positive influence for yourself on social media and in your social circle that will keep you immersed in the messages and topics you want your life to be about these days.

Cleaning out your phone contacts and social media contacts to eliminate people who are actively engaged in the lifestyle you are trying to recover from is an important part of building a pro-recovery world. Now you have space in your life to devote to people who inspire and motivate you, and to receive messages that reinforce your reasons for recovery. When you purposely follow social media accounts that promote sober living, mental and physical health, and other things you care about, you'll be exposing yourself daily to positive role models and reminders of pro-recovery messages.

LIFE HACKS
FOR EVERYDAY RELAPSE PREVENTION

Here are some simple ways to set yourself up for successful recovery in everyday life. While there is no way to guarantee that you will never have urges to relapse, you can take action to protect yourself and build resilience.

Clean up your connections.

If you haven't already done so, go through the contacts in your phone, e-mail, and on social media. Delete anyone who has provided access to drugs or alcohol in the past, like a dealer, and block or unfollow anyone on social media who glamorizes drinking or getting high, or who gives you urges to use. If you need support, ask a friend, therapist, or sponsor to help you do this.

Make it easy to access your support system.

Put them in your "favorites" list on your phone, and establish regular plans to see these people, such as weekly dinner dates or phone calls. Building recovery-focused activities into your weekly routine can help you stay accountable, so decide what fits in best for you. This can include regularly attending 12-step meetings, groups, or therapy.

Have a backup plan for the tough times.

Identify places where you feel safe, such as at a certain family member or friend's house, treatment center, or your therapist's office. Do a little research on the services in your area. Track down some hospitals, inpatient programs, and mental health clinics so that you know exactly how to get there. In the case of really strong urges, go to one of these safe places and get some support. If you know a high-risk time is coming up, like a weekend or holiday, plan to spend it at one of these places if possible.

Schedule a relapse-prevention check-in every two to four weeks.

If you work with a case manager, social worker, therapist, or sponsor, ask them to sit down with you every few weeks to do a check-in on how well your relapse-prevention plan is working. Debrief on any risky situations you've been in lately, how you handled them, and what you could have done differently. Talk about upcoming events and situations that might be difficult, and explore what will help you going into those experiences.

Revise your plan as needed.

You created a detailed relapse-prevention plan in chapter 6 (page 101), based on what's currently happening in your life, but those things may not be relevant forever. It is natural for our needs and priorities to shift as we move through life, so your relapse-prevention plan should grow and change with you. The skills and tools you find helpful today may not be the ones you turn to 10 years from now. Treat your plan as flexible, and know that you can change it based on what works best at different times in your life.

At the end of the day, you make your own decisions, including the decision to drink or use drugs. No amount of support, therapy, or planned coping strategies alone will prevent your relapsing. You have the ultimate responsibility for your actions.

Following these tips will help slow you down enough in the face of any urges to relapse, so that you can make a different choice, but it is still up to you to make the choice to stay sober.

RELAPSE AS A LEARNING OPPORTUNITY

For many people, hindsight is 20/20. After a relapse, they can look in the rearview mirror and clearly see the factors that led up to their decision to use. With practice, they then start to realize what is happening *while* it is happening, instead of afterward. Ideally, through insight and self-awareness they eventually learn how to recognize the factors leading to relapse *before* it happens, and then avoid going down that path.

Remember that you cannot control your thoughts or feelings, but you can control your actions. You decide whether you will ride out your urges, take yourself out of risky environments, or use distraction and relaxation skills when your brain is giving you thoughts of relapsing. If you lapse, you are the one who decides whether you will do it again and make it a pattern, or if you'll do what you need to get back on track in recovery.

A *lapse* occurs when you slip into a single incident of using behavior, whereas a *relapse* is a full-blown episode of using. Despite your best efforts, you are only human and thus vulnerable to making mistakes. Thinking of single incidences as *lapses* can take away some of the shame that might arise, and can help you resist the urge to say, "screw it!" and let go of your recovery efforts completely. You always have a choice. As soon as you notice that you have slipped into an old behavior, you can choose to let it take you down a path to even more using behaviors, or you can choose to recommit to your recovery and get back on track.

Sometimes people lapse because of a clear emotional or environmental trigger, as we have discussed in previous chapters. Being under a lot of stress, going through a major life change, experiencing a trauma, or simply feeling irritable, bored, overwhelmed, lonely, hungry, tired, or depleted can trigger a lapse in behaviors. (Remember HALT! [page 105]) Looking back at what happened and identifying what you were feeling, what you were doing, where you were, and who was there can help you see what brought it on and prepare you for what to look out for in the future.

RECOGNIZING "MINDLESS" LAPSES

There are also times when a lapse seems completely random and out of nowhere. In these cases, you may find that as time goes on you eventually realize what was happening that contributed to the lapse, even if it wasn't clear to you immediately afterward. Or you may never know why it happened. It could simply be that you fell back into an old habit. Behaviors that you rely on for a long time, often without thinking about them, become habitual and familiar, to the point that you might engage in them on autopilot.

Think about things you've been doing daily for many years, like brushing your teeth, or making the same commute to the office. They may be so automatic that you don't even remember doing them. Reaching for a drink or a drug can happen similarly, even if you haven't done it in a while. There doesn't always have to be a deeper meaning or an underlying motivator. In these situations, a mindfulness practice will help you catch yourself and recognize what you're about to do, or what you've begun doing. Using one of the strategies from this book, you might set a timer for 20 minutes and ride out the urge, distract yourself, or perhaps even recognize that you didn't actually have an urge in the first place and you were just reaching for the drug or drink out of habit. The more you bring your focus back to the present, the more easily you can correct course.

We cannot guarantee that we will never act on autopilot for the rest of our lives. After all, no one is mindfully present for all their waking hours. However, research shows that people who regularly practice mindfulness skills are less impulsive and more aware of their daily actions. Try setting an alarm for yourself to go off once per hour, reminding you to check in with your thoughts, feelings, and actions in that moment. With practice, this habit becomes more automatic, and you begin to realize when you've been "in your head" or mindlessly going through the motions of an activity. You learn to shift your focus back to the present moment more quickly, and this helps you stay aware of the little choices you are making throughout the day.

If you have lapsed or relapsed, remember that this does not undo the work you have done in recovery. In Exercise 8.2 (page 144), you'll reflect on what happened so that you can move forward with wisdom and clarity. If you have not lapsed, complete the exercise using a situation where you either had urges to use or did something that was not beneficial for your recovery.

EXERCISE 8.2 LEARNING FROM LAPSES

Think back and replay the scene of a recent lapse for yourself, then respond
to these prompts:

When did you get the urge to use? Be specific about day of the week and the
time of day.

_____

_____

Where were you?

_____

_____

Who were you with?

_____

_____

What were you doing? What were the people around you doing?

_____

_____

What was your mood earlier that day? What was your mood earlier that week?

_____

_____

How long had you experienced urges to relapse before you actually did it?

_____

_____

Did you consider doing anything else to cope with your urges? If so, what
other options did you consider?

_____

_____

As you read back over your description, reflect on what you could have done differently.

What thoughts contributed to the lapse? Can you recognize any of the unhelpful thoughts from chapter 3, or the voice of your inner critic chiming in?

_____

_____

What feelings contributed to the lapse? What pleasurable feelings were you trying to create, or what difficult feelings were you trying to get rid of?

_____

_____

What would have helped you respond to the thoughts and feelings differently, without turning to drugs/alcohol?

_____

_____

Ask yourself whether any of the following could protect you from future lapses (mark * by the ones that are true for you):

_____ Easier access to a support person

_____ An obvious, in-your-face reminder of distraction techniques for riding out urges

_____ More practice using healthy coping skills

_____ More support in your daily life

_____ Better boundaries with people who pressure you to use, or who treat you in ways that make you want to use

_____ A safe place to go when you feel urges

_____ A chance to talk to a therapist to find out what keeps driving you to use

Something else:

_____

_____

(Continued)

What would it take to do things differently next time?

_____

_____

Mistakes serve as powerful lessons. Use your responses to the questions above to better understand situations where you are vulnerable to relapse. You will start to notice red flags in your thinking patterns and emotions based on what has led you to lapse in the past. Make it a priority to work on the items you just starred in the list to reduce your risk of future lapses.

FORGIVING AND MOVING ON

Often, after we make mistakes, feelings of shame brim to the surface. Those unhelpful thought patterns from chapter 3 (page 44) show up, and our inner critic has a field day in our minds. After a lapse or relapse, your brain may start telling you all of the things you could've, should've, or would've done, making excuses, blaming yourself, or blaming other people. You may find your mind going into all-or-nothing thinking, such as telling you that you will never succeed in recovery, or that it will never get easier to get back on track. Remember that these words are just noises in your brain, not absolutes or facts. No one can predict the future, so assuming your destiny is neither accurate nor helpful.

It is natural to feel guilty, ashamed, or embarrassed after a relapse. However, you are only human. No one is perfect. Acknowledging what happened, apologizing for anything negative that happened as a result, and recommitting to your recovery are the best ways to ensure that the guilt and shame don't set up camp in your mind for the long haul. In some cases, you will be the only person impacted by your relapse. When this happens, do what is necessary to forgive yourself. Apologize to your brain and body for exposing them to substances, and then do something kind for yourself as a reminder that you intend to treat yourself with respect going forward.

Feelings of shame are enough punishment for most of us to learn from our mistakes, so you don't need to beat yourself up to prove that you regret it. This will only prolong the unhelpful thoughts and painful emotions that triggered you to use in the first place. You know from chapters 3 (page 44) and 4 (page 61) that the way you talk to yourself impacts your self-esteem and ability to make wise decisions. Encouraging yourself to behave differently going forward will have a much more positive effect on your actions than belittling yourself for being human and making mistakes. The best way to prove that you regret the choice you made is to make different choices going forward.

Also remember that you don't exist in a vacuum. You are the product of your conditioning, genetics, environment, and culture. You were instilled with beliefs early on, some helpful and others harmful. Recognizing that you are operating from a framework of various factors can help you see that your supposed shortcomings don't make you inherently worse than anyone else. Your struggles are part of what makes you human, just like everyone else. Remember that you've been doing the best you can, given the hand you've been dealt. The more you learn and grow, the more you have at your disposal for making new choices.

In examining your lapse, you need to remind yourself of these underlying factors that contributed to your original struggles with addiction. I hope this book has helped you see which life experiences shaped your belief system and outlook on the world. The motivation for your past behaviors likely came from experiences of trauma, shame, and feeling misunderstood. You may have never learned healthy ways to cope with painful feelings, or you may have been instilled with the belief that you don't deserve help or support. Your addiction was not the result of an inherent flaw in you. Because of the shame your experiences have caused, you were unable to recognize how your behaviors were destructive to yourself and others. You are working hard now to change that.

It is challenging to forgive yourself for harm you've caused yourself or other people, but it's a necessary challenge in recovery. Exercise 8.3 (page 148) is designed to support your self-forgiveness effort.

⛰ EXERCISE 8.3 LEARNING THE ART OF SELF-FORGIVENESS

To help you in your efforts to forgive yourself, consider these important reasons to do so:

- Without self-forgiveness, your shame can lead you to get defensive, make excuses for lapsing, or blame others for your behaviors.

- Acknowledging your faults without getting defensive allows you to use criticism and corrective feedback to help you improve.

- Self-forgiveness shows that you are willing to forgive others, too. You are demonstrating that it's okay to be human and make mistakes, and that you don't intend to hurt yourself or anyone else.

What mistakes are hardest to forgive yourself for?

_____

_____

_____

What beliefs, past messages, thoughts or feelings make it hard to forgive yourself for the mistakes you've listed?

_____

_____

_____

What beliefs, experiences, or feelings have taught you that you are expected to be good all of the time, or to be perfect and not make mistakes?

_____

_____

_____

Have you ever put unrealistic expectations on yourself or other people? Has someone else ever put unrealistic expectations on you? Write about those expectations here.

_____

_____

_____

To whom do you owe an apology for the mistakes you just wrote about? Include yourself and anyone who has been harmed by your actions.

_____

_____

_____

Write your apologies here:

_____

_____

_____

What will you do differently going forward, to show that you are "earning" forgiveness through your actions?

_____

_____

_____

Reflect on this exercise anytime you feel shame from your lapse creeping back up. Revisit these questions, and recognize which factors led to your mistake, who is owed an apology, and how you will demonstrate that you learned from this mistake.

One Day at A Time

As you get further along in recovery, you may have stretches of time when thoughts about drinking or drugs do not enter your mind. There may be times when your addiction feels like a distant memory, a story from a past life. In these periods, you get to reap the rewards of your hard work and confidently engage in your life. At other times, you may feel just as overwhelmed as you were in the very early stages of your recovery. Being able to meet yourself where you are each day involves having a plan for the worst-case scenario, and knowing when to use it.

WILLINGNESS TO RECOVER

The ACT concept of *willingness* is important for relapse prevention. Remember that willingness doesn't mean you like, want, or enjoy something. It just means that you'll allow it to be true in order to do something that is important to you, like maintain your health, stay out of jail, have meaningful relationships with loved ones, or keep your job. All of these things bring value to your life, and all can be threatened by using drugs or alcohol. Staying in recovery means you are willing to accept certain uncomfortable thoughts and feelings that you previously used drugs or alcohol to handle, in exchange for the ability to live a life of value. Exercise 8.4 (page 151) will help you examine your willingness and appreciate what it can do for you.

EXERCISE 8.4 EVALUATING YOUR WILLINGNESS

Take a moment to reflect on your willingness to keep engaging in recovery, and look at where you stand today.

While using drugs or alcohol, what experiences (thoughts, feelings, sensations) were you not willing to accept?

_____

_____

Today, what feelings are the most uncomfortable to experience?

_____

_____

What types of thoughts bother you the most?

_____

_____

What situations bring up these thoughts or feelings?

_____

_____

When you ride out difficult thoughts and feelings instead of turning to addictive behaviors, what happens?

_____

_____

(Continued)

How does staying sober positively impact these aspects of your life:
Financial stability

_____

_____

Work or school performance

_____

_____

Relationships

_____

_____

Health

_____

_____

Self-esteem

_____

_____

Reminding yourself of the payoff for staying sober can help you increase your *willingness* to handle life without using drugs or alcohol, even when life is tough, stressful, or painful. Use this exercise again in times where you feel triggered to drink or get high, to remember why your hard work is worthwhile.

MAINTAINING BALANCE IN A
PRO-RECOVERY LIFESTYLE

People become stressed—and vulnerable to doing something impulsive—when their lives are imbalanced. In chapter 7 (page 120), you learned various ways to evaluate balance in your life: through investment in self-care activities; managing basic needs such as sleep, exercise, and nutrition; and exploring your personal values to engage in values-guided behaviors every day.

When you take the time to reflect on where you are devoting your energy and resources, it becomes easier to recognize when things are out of whack, and to know what areas you've been neglecting. Conversely, when you are devoting energy to work, hobbies, social life, intimate relationships, health and self-care, spirituality, and whatever else is important to you, stress tends to be more easily managed.

Remember to do whatever you can to stay surrounded by role models, people who share your values, and messages that encourage and empower you. Regularly check in with yourself about who is in your circle, both in person and online; this will help you evaluate whether you have inadvertently allowed any toxic influences to enter your space—and to respond accordingly.

Tips and Strategies for Preventing Relapse

- Write down your relapse triggers, including people, places, and things that increase your urges or make you more likely to relapse. Come up with strategies for managing each one.

- Stop or limit contact with anyone who does not respect your recovery or who could provide you with access to your substance of choice.

- Stay connected to your support system through regular check-ins, meetings, and social activities.

- Build routines around recovery, such as support groups, 12-step meetings, or coffee dates with recovery friends.

- Sprinkle reminders of what you've gained from recovery into your daily life. Keep photos of fun memories you've created while sober, make a bucket list of places you want to see and things you want to do in your life, and spend time cultivating the relationships you missed out on during your addiction.

- Develop a gratitude practice, where you document something you appreciate about your life each day.

Trusting Your Inner Wisdom

I hope at this point you've gained a strong foundation of insight, skills, and tools for handling the ups and downs of life as a human. However, completing this workbook doesn't mean you are done with the journey.

Life will be messy as ever. You'll have joyful times and moments to celebrate, and you'll face challenges and losses. It is up to you to stay the course, to enlist support when needed, and to take pauses along the way to check what's going on in your brain, heart, and body. Recovery is not linear for anybody. At times, you will struggle again, and that's natural. Whenever you feel unsteady, go back to the sections you've found most helpful. Rework the exercises. Revisit the sidebars and bullet lists to refresh yourself on quick tips and strategies. Keep photos of the most helpful parts, so that you literally carry these tools with you in daily life.

As you stay alert to signs of impending relapse and respond with clarity, you'll find that the positive times in your life are even more rewarding, and the difficult times become more manageable without the added pain of a relapse. You're only human, and humans make mistakes. Armed with this knowledge, you are ready to gain insights if a relapse does occur, then forgive yourself and reinvest in your recovery. Mistakes and flaws do not make you wrong. They simply happened when you were disconnected from yourself.

At the end of this workbook (page 159), you'll find some helpful resources to support various aspects of your recovery. The Resources section includes directories for finding a therapist or support group, websites about addiction and mental illness, crisis hotlines for support during urges to behave in ways that are harmful, pro-recovery podcasts, and tools and apps to round out your collection of coping skills, including suggestions for guided meditations and gratitude journals. Explore these resources and know that there are many others out there, designed to help you thrive.

In her book *True Refuge: Finding Peace and Freedom in Your Own Awakened Heart*, psychologist and meditation teacher Tara Brach points to the natural wisdom inside each of us: "The biggest illusion about a path of refuge is that we are on our way somewhere else, on our way to becoming a different kind of person. But ultimately, our refuge is not outside ourselves, not somewhere in the future—it is always and already here."

Trust that in any given moment you have the ability to pause and look inward to find inner stability. Your core values provide guidance for how to behave in life. Thoughts, feelings, and urges will come and go, but at your core live the values and qualities that make you *you*. If you pause to cut through the noise of those thoughts, cravings, and emotions, you can hear your inner wisdom, guiding you to freedom and peace.

RESOURCES

Alcoholics Anonymous (AA): AA.org

Al-Anon and Alateen: Al-Anon.org

National Alliance on Mental Illness (NAMI): NAMI.org

National Council on Alcoholism and Drug Dependence (NCADD):
NCADD.org

Substance Abuse and Mental Health Services Administration (SAMHSA):
SAMHSA.gov

APPS, MEDITATIONS, AND GUIDED IMAGERY

Applications for Smartphones and Devices:

Grateful: A Gratitude Journal is an app with daily prompts for documenting your gratitude, writing down positive moments and things you appreciate. It is available in free or paid versions on iTunes or the App Store.

Calm Harm is an app for handling urges to self-harm and coping with distress, available for free on Google Play or the App Store.

Headspace is a meditation and mindfulness app that teaches beginners to meditate in short, manageable steps. It can also be used as part of an ongoing mindfulness practice. Available in free or paid versions on the App Store or Google Play.

Guided Imagery and Guided Meditations:

Health Journeys Guided Imagery is an audio-based guided imagery designed specifically as a relaxation tool for listeners recovering from addictions: HealthJourneys.com/audio-library/addictions-compulsive-behavior

Tara Brach's Guided Meditations cover a variety of topics and are focused on increasing inner peace: TaraBrach.com/guided-meditations

PODCASTS ABOUT ADDICTION RECOVERY

The Bubble Hour: BlogTalkRadio.com/BubbleHour

Clean and Sober Radio: CleanAndSoberBroadcasting.com

A Mindful Emergence: WPVMFM.org/show/a-mindful-emergence-2

That Sober Guy: Stitcher.com/podcast/that-sober-guy-podcast

BOOKS

There are many books in this large and growing field; I've included here a few that my clients and I have found most helpful, but I encourage you to explore what's out there and ask your recovery team for their recommendations.

The Addictive Personality: Understanding the Addictive Process and Compulsive Behavior by Craig Nakken

The Assertiveness Workbook: How to Express Your Ideas and Stand Up for Yourself at Work and in Relationships by Randy J. Paterson

Freedom from Anxious Thoughts and Feelings by Scott Symington

Invisible Heroes: Survivors of Trauma and How They Heal by Belleruth Naparstek

Overcoming Unwanted Intrusive Thoughts: A CBT-Based Guide to Getting Over Frightening, Obsessive, or Disturbing Thoughts by Sally M. Winston and Martin N. Seif

Trauma and Recovery: The Aftermath of Violence—From Domestic Abuse to Political Terror by Judith L. Herman

DIRECTORIES FOR FINDING A MENTAL HEALTH/ADDICTION PROFESSIONAL

American Psychological Association—Find a Psychologist: Locator.APA.org

EMDR Therapist Network: EMDRTherapistNetwork.com

Good Therapy: GoodTherapy.org

Psychology Today: PsychologyToday.com

Talkspace (online and text therapy): TalkSpace.com

Trauma-Focused Cognitive Behavioral Therapy: TFCBT.org/members

HOTLINES

Hotlines for Crisis Support

If you are ever in danger or experiencing a crisis that requires immediate assistance, dial 911 or go to the nearest emergency room.

Hotlines for Addiction Crisis Support

National Alliance on Mental Illness (NAMI) Crisis Text Line: Text START to 741741 to receive 24/7 text message crisis support for mental health or substance abuse crises.

Substance Abuse and Mental Health Services Administration (SAMHSA) National Helpline: 1-800-662-HELP (1-800-662-4357) information service available in English and Spanish for individuals and family members facing mental health and/or substance use disorders. Call for referrals to local treatment facilities, support groups, and community organizations. Call or visit their website for free publications and guides.

Hotlines for Self-Harm and Suicide

International Suicide Prevention Wiki provides a worldwide directory of suicide prevention hotlines, online chats, text lines, and resources at SuicidePrevention.wikia.com

National Suicide Prevention Lifeline: 1-800-273-TALK (1-800-273-8255) for 24/7 free confidential support and resources. Also available online at SuicidePreventionLifeline.org

Self-Harm Prevention Hotline: 1-800-DON'T-CUT (1-800-366-8288) or visit online at SelfInjury.com

Hotlines for Violence and Assault

National Domestic Violence Hotline: 800-799-SAFE (800-799-7233) for 24/7 confidential support in English or Spanish for anyone experiencing or recovering from domestic violence.

National Sexual Assault Hotline: 800-656-HOPE (800-656-4673)

SOCIAL MEDIA

Follow **hashtags** that promote recovery, including:

#AddictionRecovery

#AlcoholismRecovery

#AddictionTreatment

#DrugFree

#DrugFreeLife

#RecoveryWarrior

#Sober

#SoberLife

Follow social media accounts for treatment centers and organizations that promote recovery, such as:

Alcoholics Anonymous (regional and local chapters)

Hazelden Betty Ford Foundation (@HazeldenBettyFord)

National Alliance on Mental Illness (@NAMICommunicate) and NAMI local chapters

Recovery Today Magazine (@RecoveryTodayMag)

REFERENCES

"Adult Children of Alcoholics." Cornell College. Accessed July 11, 2018. https://www.cornellcollege.edu/counseling/student-resources/acoa.shtml.

Afkar, Abolhasan, Seyed M. Rezvani, and Abdolhosein E. Sigaroudi. "Measurement of Factors Influencing the Relapse of Addiction: A Factor Analysis." *International Journal of High Risk Behaviors and Addiction* 6, no. 3 (2016). doi: 10.5812/ijhrba.32141.

Alcoholics Anonymous (AA) World Services. "What is AA?" https://www.aa.org/pages/en_US/what-is-aa Accessed July 1, 2018.

American Addiction Centers. "The Link Between PTSD and Substance Abuse/Addiction." Accessed August 1, 2018. https://americanaddictioncenters.org/ptsd.

Beck, Aaron T. *Cognitive Therapy and the Emotional Disorders*. New York, NY: The Penguin Group, 1979.

Beck, Judith S. *Cognitive Behavior Therapy: Basics and Beyond*, 2nd ed. New York, NY: The Guilford Press, 2011.

Brach, Tara. *True Refuge: Finding Peace and Freedom in Your Own Awakened Heart*. New York, NY: Bantam, 2013.

Brown, Brené. *The Gifts of Imperfection*. Center City, MN: Hazelden Publishing, 2010.

Burns, David D. *The Feeling Good Handbook*. Plume, 1999.

Clay, Rebecca A. "The Link Between Food and Mental Health." *APA Monitor on Psychology* 48, no. 8 (2017). http://www.apa.org/monitor/2017/09/food-mental-health.aspx.

Diagnostic and Statistical Manual of Mental Disorders (5th Ed). Washington, DC: American Psychiatric Association, 2013.

Engel, Beverly. "Healing Your Shame and Guilt Through Self-Forgiveness." *Psychology Today*, 2017. Accessed August 18, 2018. https://www.psychologytoday.com/us/blog the-compassion-chronicles/201706/healing-your-shame-and-guilt-through-self-forgiveness.

Harris, Russ. *The Happiness Trap: Stop Struggling, Start Living*. Sydney: Read How You Want/Accessible, 2014.

Johns Hopkins Medicine. "Substance Abuse/Chemical Dependency." The Johns Hopkins University. Accessed July 1, 2018. https://www.hopkinsmedicine.org/healthlibrary/conditions/adult/mental_health_disorders/substance_abuse_or_chemical_dependence_85,p00761.

Luoma, Jason B., et al. "An Investigation of Stigma in Individuals Receiving Treatment for Substance Abuse." *Addictive Behaviors* 32, no. 7 (2007): 1331–46. doi10.1016/j.addbeh.2006.09.008.

Mancebo, M. C., et al. "Substance Use Disorders in an Obsessive Compulsive Disorder Clinical Sample." *Journal of Anxiety Disorders* 23, no. 4 (2009): 429-35. doi: http://doi.org/10.1016/j.janxdis.2008.08.008.

McCauley, J. L., T. Killeen, D. F. Gros, K. T. Brady, and S. E. Back. "Posttraumatic Stress Disorder and Co-Occurring Substance Use Disorders: Advances in Assessment and Treatment." *Clinical Psychology* 19, no. 3. (2012). doi: http://doi.org/10.1111/cpsp.12006.

Miller, Leah. "Drug Relapse Prevention Tips." *Project Know: An American Addiction Centers Resource*. Accessed July 21, 2018. https://www.project-know.com/research/relapse-prevention.

Montano, C. B. "Recognition and Treatment of Depression in a Primary Care Setting." *Journal of Clinical Psychiatry*, (1994). https://www.ncbi.nlm.nih.gov/pubmed/7814355.

Najavits, Lisa M. *Seeking Safety: A Treatment Manual for PTSD and Substance Abuse*. New York: Guilford Press, 2001.

National Eating Disorders Association. "Substance Abuse and Eating Disorders." Accessed August 1, 2018. https://www.nationaleatingdisorders.org/substance-abuse-and-eating-disorders.

National Heart, Lung, and Blood Institute. "Sleep Deprivation and Deficiency." Accessed July 23, 2018. https://www.nhlbi.nih.gov/health-topics/sleep-deprivation-and-deficiency.

Neff, Kristin. *Self-Compassion: The Proven Power of Being Kind to Yourself*. HarperCollins Publishers, 2011.

NIDA. "Treatment Approaches for Drug Addiction." *National Institute on Drug Abuse* (January 17, 2018). Accessed July 1, 2018. https://www.drugabuse.gov/publications/drugfacts/treatment-approaches-drug-addiction.

Paterson, Randy. *The Assertiveness Workbook: How To Express Your Ideas and Stand Up For Yourself At Work and in Relationships*. Oakland, CA: New Harbinger Publications, 2000.

Portland Psychotherapy Team. "Riding the Wave: Using Mindfulness to Help Cope With Urges." Portland Psychotherapy Clinic. Accessed August 11, 2018. https://portlandpsychotherapyclinic.com/2011/11/riding-wave-using-mindfulness-help-cope-urges.

Prochaska, and J. Q, and C. C. DiClemente. *The Transtheoretical Approach: Crossing Traditional Boundaries of Change*. Homewood, IL: Dorsey Press, 1984.

Salo, Ruth, et al. "Psychiatric Comorbidity in Methamphetamine Dependence." *Psychiatry Research* 186, nos. 2–3 (2011): 356–61. Accessed August 1, 2018.

Snow, D., and C. Anderson. "Exploring the Factors Influencing Relapse and Recovery among Drug and Alcohol Addicted Women." *Journal of Psychosocial Nursing and Mental Health Services* 38, no. 7 (2000): 8–19. https://www.ncbi.nlm.nih.gov/pubmed/10911586.

"Substance Abuse Treatment for Persons With Co-Occurring Disorders: A Treatment Improvement Protocol." https://store.samhsa.gov/system/files/sma13-3992.pdf.

"Toxic Stress." Center on the Developing Child, Harvard University. Accessed July 11, 2018. https://developingchild.harvard.edu/science/key-concepts/toxic-stress.

Vowles, Kevin E., and John T. Sorrell. "Life with Chronic Pain: An Acceptance-Based Approach." Centre for Pain Research, School for Health, University of Bath & San Mateo Medical Center, Clinical Trials and Research & VA Palo Alto Health Care System, Center for Health Care Evaluation, July 2007.

Walker, Pete. "The 4Fs: A Trauma Typology in Complex PTSD." *The East Bay Therapist*, 2003. www.pete-walker.com/fourFs_TraumaTypologyComplexPTSD.htm.

INDEX

ACKNOWLEDGMENTS

FIRST, I WOULD LIKE to thank the patients I have had the honor of working with over the past several years. I have learned profound lessons in witnessing their bravery and resilience. I would like to acknowledge those who have valiantly battled their addictions and lost their lives in the process. I honor your memory in the work I do every day.

I am grateful for the supportive training environments and treatment centers where I cut my teeth as a clinician, and the supervisors and mentors who guided my professional development—most notably, Jennifer Schmidt, Neil Bockian, Jeff Gottlieb, Mark Miller, and Alison Sharpe-Havill. A special thank-you is reserved for Uri Heller, for his long-term mentorship, support, and friendship. He has been an endless source of wisdom and humor. Thanks to Melissa Valentine for her patience and valuable feedback throughout this process.

Thank you to Donna Freedman and Joel Freedman for instilling me with deep compassion for my fellow humans, and for far more than I could put into a single paragraph. Finally, thank you to Jeremy Diamond, for giving me confidence when I most needed it, and for forcing me to take writing breaks whenever I became a frazzled, unwashed hermit.

ABOUT THE AUTHOR

 **PAULA A. FREEDMAN, PSYD,** is a clinical psychologist who specializes in anxiety disorders, addiction, and eating disorders. She has worked in a variety of settings, including community mental health clinics, schools, hospitals, and chemical dependency treatment centers. She currently provides individual and group therapy in her private practice. She enjoys helping her clients connect with their inner wisdom in everyday life. Dr. Freedman lives in Chicago, Illinois, with her husband and dog.

CPSIA information can be obtained
at www.ICGtesting.com
Printed in the USA
BVHW060548210519
548809BV00001B/1/P

9 781641 521178